I Just Called Her Momma

Mae Durden-Nelson

SUNBELT EAKIN Austin, Texas

FIRST EDITION

Published in the U.S.A.
By Sunbelt Eakin Press
A Division of Sunbelt Media, Inc.
P.O. Drawer 90159
Austin, Texas 78709-0159
email: sales@eakinpress.com
website: www.eakinpress.com

1 2 3 4 5 6 7 8 9
1-57168-714-9

Library of Congress Cataloging-in-Publication Data

Durden-Nelson, Mae
I just called her Momma / Mae Durden-Nelson.– 1st ed.
p. cm.
ISBN 1-57168-714-9
1. Durden-Nelson, Mae, 1932–Childhood and youth–Juvenile literature. 2. Farmers–Texas–Gillespie County–Biography–Juvenile literature. 3. Farm life–Texas–Gillespie County–Juvenile literature. 4. German Americans–Texas–Gillespie County–Juvenile literature. 5. Gillespie County (Tex.)–Biography–Juvenile literature. I. Title
CT275.D8845A3 2003
976.4'65062'092–dc21 2002156355

You gave inspiration for this book:

Nancy Clara (Hahn) Ippolito
(my Godchild and niece)
and her child
Anna Clara Ippolito

This book is also dedicated to every young person
who will read all the pages of this book.
And,
if some curious adult should happen to
pick it up and actually read it through,
I hope you will hug your child
and tell them how precious they really, really are!

—Mae Durden-Nelson

Contents

Foreword

As I look out of my kitchen window, I can see the house across a wide span of fields where the author of this book grew up. Not only have I known Alora Mae ever since she was born, but also, a warm friendship based on mutual respect and admiration has existed between our families going back in time to when our mothers were growing up and, as teenagers, exchanged friendship cards through the local post office, then located at Lange's Mill near Doss, Texas.

Throughout the fleeting years, one accumulates many pleasant memories, but among them the most impressionable ones are formed during the innocence of childhood—especially if they were experienced at a time when the peace and tranquility of a simple rural life kept the family closely knit together, and the outside world was far removed.

On a small farm, such as the one where Alora Mae grew up, the land had been carved out of a pristine wilderness by clearing trees and brush—by hand labor—in order to prepare fields for growing crops. The farmer worked diligently to create a subsistence lifestyle by planting gardens, and canning vegetables and fruits; milking cows to have milk, butter, cream and cheese; raising chickens for meat and eggs and hogs to provide bacon, ham and sausage. They would only need to buy staples such as sugar, flour, and salt whenever they made the long trip to the small "Mom and Pop" grocery stores in Fredericksburg.

There was also the Depression of the early thirties, when money was scarce and parents could not provide for all the wants and desires of their children.

The author, Alora Mae, still experienced the more simple lifestyle—attending the small rural school in Doss, the little country church and Sunday school and participating in the social life of a community.

It was these precious memories of a warm and loving relationship within a hard-working family of high morals and integrity that prompted the author to share a portion of them with you. Enjoy!

—Mrs. Edna (Miss Edna) Crenwelge
Doss, Texas

Mrs. Edna Crenwelge, affectionately known as "Miss Edna" to the countless students she taught at the Doss Common School District.

— Permission by Mrs. Edna Crenwelge

Acknowledgments

To all those who have helped me along the way: To Bill Nelson, my awesome motivator architect husband, who helped me design my story; my siblings, Bernice Dittmar, Otto Hahn Jr., Warren Hahn, and Helen Hahn (sister-in-law), your memories and stories are precious; Ms. Irene Spenrath, gentle lady and head librarian, my mentor and friend for thirty years, for always encouraging me to believe in myself at the Comfort Independent School District; Ms. Edna Crenwelge, an amazing teacher, who touched and influenced countless students in the Doss Common School District; Mary Sansom, a retired second grade teacher/friend, for her wonderful "can do" spirit and help; and special kudos to my three levelheaded sons, Don, James, and Roger Durden, who didn't let me quit even when life seemed at its darkest; and Carmen Richardson, an incredible teacher and reviewer.

Also to all the children who illuminated my life for twenty-seven years in the Comfort Elementary Library. Storytime with you was a daily adventure! Your love of books and reading inspired my librarian's work and made it seem like play.

To the staff; Ellen Collie, Carol Borcherding, Cathy Behrens, Susan Durden, Marcia Habecker, Anna Bennett, Jane O'Brian, Tana Keyhoe, Larry McQuay, Debbie Bosworth, Patti Cox, Kim

Bolin, Mary Helen Sibley, Ginger Derr, Linda Lich, Kit Nelson, Ruth Coffey, Kathy Masser, Virginia Milner, Audell Burkey, Senaida Castro, Mary Houghton, Mac Anderson, Liz Magee, Paula Russ, Sandra Hicks, Dora McKeithan, Earl McKeithan, Caroll Bell and admininstators, Neil Bergmann, Ken Peterman, and Connie Spenrath, you daily lifted my goals to greater heights. Especially Mr. Eddie Derr, superintendent, for standing behind our elementary library and helping to make it one of the finest in the state. And finally, to Mark Davis, a fellow struggling writer, a born teacher who gave me the courage to automate our library, and always a friend through thick and thin.

Thank you all.

Chapter One

Of Secrets and Snoring

It all began when Momma turned down the wick on the kerosene lamp. It made my bedroom so dim all I could see was Momma's face. She had just tucked me into bed, had told me good night and was about to leave my room.

"Momma?" I sat up in my bed and grasped her hand. "Could you just stay with me for a little while?"

"*Was jetzt?*" (What now?)

"Just . . . talk to me, please?"

"*Puppe, deine Mutter ist sehr müde*" (You mother is very tired.) "We were up so late last night at your sister's wedding and then the reception . . ."

"Momma?"

"*Ja.*"

"Would you sleep with me tonight, please?"

"*Nein, nein, Puppe.* You be a big girl for Momma tonight. You're six years old and you are so lucky to have this big bed all to yourself now. How about that?"

The coal oil lamp was the source of light for the Hahn family during the early years of the author's life. Washing the fragile glass chimney was extrememly dangerous and was a daily chore for Momma.

— From the Susan Rose Durden collection, Comfort, Texas

"I wish Bernice was not married. I liked it when she slept by me."

"*Ja. Ja* ... We'll talk about that tomorrow. You go to sleep now. Your daddy and your three brothers are already sound asleep. If you'll listen real close, I bet you can hear them all snore a different song. Isn't that funny?"

I managed a small smile. "*Ja,* Momma. I'll try."

Momma left my room carrying the darkened lamp and gently closed my door.

Now it really was dark! It was like the inside of my closet when I crawl inside to hide from Warren, my little brother. I closed my eyes and squeezed them shut tight. *Go to sleep,* I told myself. *Listen. Can you hear them snore ...*

Something hit the window screen. My eyes opened wide. Even though I stared at the window, I couldn't see anything—it was that black.

There—there it is again! It could be a big bug—maybe. Oh no—*no! There's something out there—and it knows I'm alone.*

No! I will not be afraid. Just because Bernice is not here—and I'm sleeping alone for the first time—in my whole life!

But, there it is again! Someone is scratching on the screen! And—there's a cellar under my floor. What if someone—or something—comes in here and eats me—and Momma won't even hear—and ...

I pull the sheet up under my chin even though it is June and very warm. I can hear the katydids—there must be a million of them. I grit my teeth. I hold my breath and strain my ears to see if I can detect anything. And then I do!

There is something at the other window too!

There are four windows in my room and they're all wide open. Oh, no. Now there's a shadow outside—I can just barely see it. It's moving. There's a queen's crown on a trellis outside those windows. Maybe someone is hiding behind it and ... My heart is going kerthunp, kerthump—I can hear it.

"Momma. Momma." My voice sounds strange—like it belongs to someone else. I must call louder. I keep trying, "Momma. MOMMA."

At last. Momma opens my door holding the lighted kerosene lamp in her other hand. I am gasping—trying to catch my breath. "Momma, there's something outside my window. It made a noise on the screen and—"

"Oh, *Puppe,* there is nothing outside that would harm you."

"Momma. I heard it and there's something behind those vines—"

I began to whimper as I was speaking.

"Shhh, *Puppe. Puppe.*" Momma put her arms around me. It was amazing how safe I felt then.

"Don't cry anymore. Move over. I'll sleep with you. Papa is snoring pretty bad anyway. Maybe this way I'll get some sleep."

"*Danke schön,* Momma. I will sleep now too and I promise, I'll not snore."

"*Bitte schön, meine kleine Alora.* Nobody snores like papa does. You ought to hear him. He snores like this." Momma made funny snoring sounds with whistles in-between.

"Like this, Momma?" I tried to imitate her snoring sounds, but I got the giggles so bad I couldn't finish.

I guess we both fell sound asleep. It seemed only a little while later when I awoke to our roosters' crowing. Momma was already up. I could hear her in the kitchen and smell bacon frying. *I better get out of bed.*

Nobody misses breakfast at our house. Today there will only be six people at the table. I wonder where Bernice is this morning and if she missed me last night as much as I missed her. Oh, well, she's married, so I guess she'll sleep with Arthur now. Yuck. He has a mustache. Yuck. Sister always laughs when he kisses her. I guess it tickles. He tried to kiss me once. I ducked away from him . . .

"*Puppe.* Time for breakfast."

I better go when Momma calls. I'm glad Momma came last night when I called.

"*Ja,* Momma. I'm coming."

I jumped out of bed and hurried to pull off my long soft white nightgown. I hung it on the inside of my closet door—and I was reminded how dark it was last night. I stepped inside the closet and pulled the door shut. Ah ha. That's exactly how dark it was last night. I quickly opened the door and stepped out into my room. I wondered if I could find a flashlight to take to bed with me tonight. I hope Momma doesn't mention at breakfast how scared I was last night. My brothers will tease me bad—especially Oliver. I hate that.

"*Puppe!* Are you coming? I need you to set the table!"

"*Ja,* Momma, right away." I pulled on my dress—the same one I've worn all week. Momma made it for me out of chicken feed sacks. I love it a lot. It has these circles all over it—all different colors. Daddy let me pick it out myself when we had to buy chicken feed. It takes two feed sacks to make one dress for me. Momma and I always have fun making up a pattern for my dresses. Especially this one. She let me look in her button box to see how many buttons I can find to match. That's why this dress was so much fun. I found buttons to match all the circles—except the yellow. Momma bought a card of yellow buttons at the store in Fredericksburg. Momma showed me how to sew on the buttons myself—one in each circle . . .

"*Puppe!* Did you go back to sleep? I don't want to call you again!"

"No, Momma. I'm coming. I'm running." The floor felt cool under my bare feet. I love summertime—no shoes—except on Sunday.

"Good morning, Momma! Will we eat out on the screened porch?"

"*Ja, ja—aber mach jetzt schnell.* Papa wants to get an early start in the field today. Did you wash your hands?"

"Yes, Momma, I will." I quickly washed my hands under the sink faucet—brrr, the water is so cold. I wish we had hot running water like Uncle Felix.

I set places for six at the table. I called out to Momma in the kitchen next to our porch, "Momma? Don't tell Papa and the boys about me being scared last night, please?"

"Of course not. It's none of their business. Sometimes us girls just have to keep our secrets. Did you know that you snored last night, Alora?"

"Momma, you're teasing me—I didn't snore."

"How do you know you didn't?"

I'm glad the boys and daddy showed up about then so I didn't have to answer Momma. How do you know if you snore or not? I wonder if Art snores. Bernice will be sorry she got married then.

Chapter Two

Momma Makes a Promise

My sister and I shared our bedroom until June 1938, when she married and moved away. Everybody was so excited because she married a University of Texas graduate with a degree in physics. I don't know what physics is, and I sure have never been to Austin, where the college is. All I do know is that he took my big sister away and now I have to sleep alone in our room. It is separated from my parents' bedroom by only a short hallway, but I feel Momma is miles away. Every night it's the same ordeal: I get scared. I cry. Momma crawls in bed with me.

One morning, Momma awoke me before she went to the kitchen.

You ought to see my momma's thick black hair. It has grown to below her waist. One does not see her like that often because every morning when she gets out of bed, she brushes it real fast, then reaches back with both hands, gathers her hair together, and switches it round and round until it is like a rope. Then, she rolls it up into a ball in the back of her head and holds it there under her left hand while she pins it in place with hairpins with her right hand. In German she calls it a *Ditzel*. Momma always wears her hair like that.

I have never seen it any other way. She allows me to hand her the hairpins this morning. I feel in a playful mood and don't hand her the last pin. Boy! She noticed immediately and laughingly scolds me in German, "*Du bist eine kleine taugen nichts!*" (You are a little prankster.) Momma gives me a big hug and pats my leg.

"Hurry now. Get up and get dressed."

Momma has a pretty face. She has much smoother skin than most of the other farm wives. She seldom goes out into the hot sun to work in the fields like most of her friends. I complain about that sometimes, saying I'd like to go outside to work with Daddy and my brothers. But she says, "I need you to stay indoors with me and learn to do housework." Most of the time I don't mind.

Momma never wears lipstick or any kind of makeup. None of her farm women friends do. And, except for an Elgin gold wristwatch on Sundays when we go to church, she never wears jewelry either. That's not because she has anything against jewelry. When I asked her about that once she just laughed and said, "It's not important." I have seen a picture of her when she was a twenty-year-old girl. She wore jewelry then—lots of it.

My mother's maiden name was Clara Emilia Lange, but when she married Papa her last name changed to Hahn. I just call her Momma.

Both my parents are descendents of German immigrants, and they grew up living about four miles apart. They were married September 20, 1920, after World War I was over. There are five siblings in my family. My sister, Bernice, the oldest, was born in June 1921. Her given name is Bernice Lena Hulda Hahn. She was named after both our grandmothers. She hates her two middle names. I don't know why.

Next is my brother, Otto Jr., born in 1923. He was named after my papa. Another brother, Oliver, was born in 1930; then me,

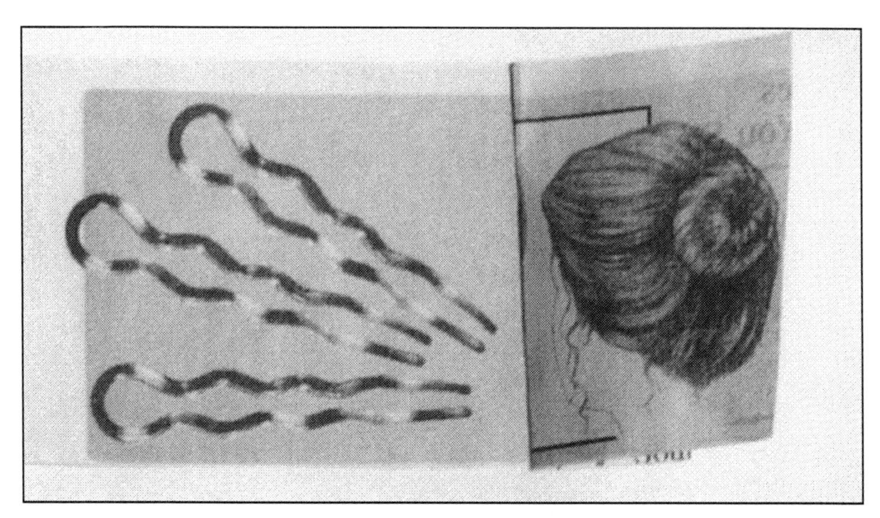

This was the hairstyle Momma wore. A time-saving style as she nurtured her family of five children. It is know as a "bun." In Momma's Germany, it was called a "Ditzel."

Alora, in 1932. The last child was born in 1934. My "little" brother, Warren, weighed twelve pounds at birth!

My family lives on a small farm in the central part of Texas in Gillespie County. It was acquired for Papa with a down payment made by my grandfather Fredrick Hahn in 1918 while Daddy was in France during World War I. When Daddy came home after the war was over, he and Momma were married. This 650-acre farm became their home, and they've never lived anyplace else. Momma and Daddy paid off the prime land at two dollars an acre.

I love our farm, but every night it is the same distress: I crawl into my bed and pull the covers up to my chin—even though it is very warm. Before long I just *know* somebody is either hiding under my bed or I just *know* something is going to come and *get* me and my momma won't even hear. I try really, really hard not to be afraid because by now my brothers have found out what's going on with me and they never miss an opportunity to tease me. They are calling me a baby, or in German they say I'm an *angst schisser,* which is really *naughty!* Of course they won't say that to me when Momma or Daddy are around because they would get into a ton of trouble.

I ought to tattle on them, but I'm having enough trouble. So, I just stick out my tongue at them and go on about my business.

I am trying really hard to not be so afraid. But before I know it, I begin to whimper softly. When Momma does not come, I get louder and louder until finally she appears wearing her long white nightgown, her hair hanging down for the night. She has the appearance of an angel standing there in the doorway, carrying a kerosene lamp. She comes over to my bed, sets the lamp on the nightstand, and sits on the edge of my mattress. Each time she asks me what is wrong. All I can say is, "I'm scared to sleep alone, Momma."

Momma just sighs, shakes her head, and crawls into bed with me and I go to sleep. Funny how I feel so protected and safe then.

After almost two weeks, one morning Momma asked, "Would you feel better if we fixed up or changed around your room? You're such a big girl now and pretty smart too."

"What do you mean, Momma? Fix up my room?"

"That's up to you," Momma said. "We can do almost anything if it doesn't cost too much money. You think about it. You decide."

"Could we make it a princess's bedroom? No princess would be afraid to sleep in her very own special bedroom." I amazed myself with that idea. I don't know where it came from.

"That's a wonderful idea. What would we need to do?"

I shrugged my shoulders. "I don't know, Momma. I have to think about it."

"You do that and when you figure it out, let me know and we'll see what we can do."

I spent a lot of time that day looking for ideas in our Sears and Roebuck mail-order catalog. I found lots of pretty curtains for the windows, but our curtains were almost new. I turned the pages slowly; there were lots of things I didn't have. There were dressers with mirrors and then—wow! I found *something,* all right.

"Momma! Momma!" I yelled and ran to the kitchen. "Look!"

Momma went to her rocking chair in the living room and sat down. I laid the big thick catalog in her lap.

"A blue satin headboard? *Ist das nicht schön!*"

"Oh, Momma, if I had that kind of bed I could rub my hands on it at night and maybe I wouldn't be so scared."

"*Ja. Ja.* That could be. Sometimes it helps to have something soft and smooth and pretty to touch."

But Momma's eyes clouded. As she studied the picture, a sad look came into her face. She glanced at me, then looked away and spoke softly as she her hand caressed my hair.

"Oh, *meine kleine Puppe.* I'm afraid that headboard costs too much money."

I knew that's what Momma'd say. I am used to hearing "*It costs too much money.*" Momma and Daddy say it often. They say it's the *Depression.*

I don't know what that means, but I've decided it must be something really bad. Because every time they say that word *depression,* they always shake their heads and look down at the ground. Then they take a deep breath, straighten up, and lift their heads, nodding gently like they just decided something special. "We're going to be all right. We just have to work a little harder, that's all. Yes. We're going to be just fine."

So, like I said, I really don't understand what *depression* means except it's hard work and no money to spend. But I've learned not to complain. It makes my momma and daddy sad when we grumble.

"That's okay, Momma. Don't look so sad. I'll keep the catalog in my room and I'll just look at it and pretend."

But no matter how hard I tried, the picture did not help me to go to sleep at night. I continued to cry for Momma. So patient with me, she continued to stay with me night after night.

A week later, while wc were again fixing breakfast, Momma asked, "*Puppe,* do you still have that picture . . . of the blue satin . . ."

"I do, Momma." I ran to get it and opened to the page. I anxiously studied Momma's face. I can tell when she's up to something. I saw that look there now.

"Why do you want to see it again, Momma?"

Momma popped her hand right on the picture and then snapped her fingers in the air.

"I've been thinking." She narrowed her eyes and nodded her head up and down. "I saw some blue satin in Fredericksburg at Norman Brothers Dry Goods Store the other day, and I'll bet, if you'll be good and work hard and help me, I think you and I will be able to *make* a headboard just like that." Momma tweaked my nose.

"But how can *we* do that, Momma?"

"I've got an idea. I've got an old quilt, some leftover cotton, and a torn sheet. We could fill in all the spaces on your headboard, cover it with a quilt and a sheet, then sew it real tight so that it won't slip down off the frame. Then, I could sew a thing out of blue satin that looks like a giant pillowcase. We'll slip it down over the headboard. It won't take much material . . ."

"But what about the big buttons, Momma?"

"I think you could find some big old buttons in my button box. We could cover them with cotton and blue satin and . . ."

"*Ja,* Momma. That'll work. I know it will. Oh, Momma. I'll work really hard and help you and—Momma, I promise, I will not cry anymore when I go to bed at night. I'm a big girl now. Right?"

Momma kneeled down so we were face to face, put her hands on my shoulders, and said, "Now, you must understand this, *Puppe.* I'll have to talk this over with Daddy. If we can find the money, you and I will work on your bed every chance we get—after our work is done."

Would my Daddy agree to buy the blue satin? I didn't really know for sure, but I was pretty confident. He is a kind, gentle man that loves his family, and I know if it is at all possible to buy that material, Momma and I will be making my headboard soon—after our work is done, of course.

Chapter Three

Molasses, Blood Sausage, and Brains

But my blue satin headboard remained only a picture in a catalog. There was no end to our work. It seems like we never ever get through. From early in the morning till it gets dark at night, there is always work, work, work. Everybody works.

My daddy is always the first one up in the morning. He fixes a fire in the wood-burning stove and then he and my oldest brother go out to milk our three cows. Meanwhile, my other brother, Oliver, two years older than I, goes out to feed the chickens and pigs and splits wood for our cook stove. The wood box behind our stove is always having to be filled, as we burn a lot of it in one day's time.

My job is to help Momma and also get my little brother Warren out of bed, help him get dressed, and wash his hands and face. How he hates the cold water.

Next, Momma has taught me to set the table on "*die Galerie.*" In summer we always eat out on the screened-in porch just off the

This 1930s modern enameled coffee pot was used daily, and Papa did the starting of it as soon as he had the morning fire going in the wood-burning stove. It heated and cooked as the stove heated and cooked—slow!

— From the Warren Hahn collection. Photo by Bill Nelson

kitchen. We all love that. In the fall and winter we eat in our dining room.

It is a rule that everybody must come to the table when the food is prepared. The only time we're not expected is when someone is ill. But nobody wants to miss mealtime. Not only is the food always good, but that's when we laugh a lot. Someone always has a funny story to tell.

Oliver, Warren, and I sit on a bench. The last one at table has to sit in the middle. Yuck. Another good reason not to be late. Warren has to sit in the middle today.

Breakfast is also when we hear conversation between Momma and Daddy. We are quiet and listen when they talk. We must not interrupt. It is usually interesting and informative. Daddy loves to tease Momma, and he won't quit until she finally says, "*Ach, Pappa, du sollst so was nicht sagen vor die Kinder.*" (Pappa, you ought not to say things like that in front of the children!")

Sometimes, we get the giggles so bad that finally Momma or Daddy will stop talking and they give us a puzzled look and ask, "*Was ist so Spaßig?*" (What is so funny?)

All three of us younger children sing out together: "*Du hast Butter an deine Nase, Pappa!*" (There's some butter on your nose.)

Finally, everybody is laughing hard . . . Daddy especially.

Breakfast is wonderful. We're having oatmeal today.

Oatmeal comes in a box labeled Mother's Oats. It is fun to watch Momma open a new container because it has either a cup and saucer or some kind of small dish in it. My favorite is a dark blue glass bowl or small plate.

Momma cooks oatmeal in a big blue-and-white enameled pot on top of our wood-burning stove. When the oatmeal is done, she empties it into a large dish and sets it in the middle of the table. Daddy is first to help himself. Then the dish is passed around the

Enameled cooking pots, the forerunner of aluminum kitchen ware, chipped easily and had to be replaced often. After aluminum proved unsatisfactory, stainless steel copper-bottomed cooking became popular. Soon was added early Pyrex glassware, which proved too breakable. It soon gave way to today's waterless cooking technology and space-age Teflon-lined pots and pans. Today there are many choices for the cook.

— From Antiques on High, Seventh and High Street, Comfort, Texas, Diane Potter.
Photo by Bill Nelson

table for each of us to take our share. Momma's always last. I can't figure how she knows how much to cook. It always comes out just right. Well, sometimes there's a little bit left over. Then our twenty kittens are happy to get it.

We also have on our table fresh cream and homemade bread and fresh yellow butter to eat with our oatmeal. Along with all that, we are having ham from our own smokehouse. Momma fries it in a black cast-iron skillet. Sometimes we have bacon. But best of all is when we have fried or boiled fresh-smoked venison/pork sausage. Our family makes a lot of venison and pork sausages every winter.

Oh. Yes. That reminds me. Sometimes in winter Momma puts cooked blood sausage on the table with our oatmeal. I never eat that! None of us kids do. We've all seen how blood sausage is made.

At butchering time, Daddy shoots the hog he's been feeding for a long time. Next, he sticks the hog in its throat with a "*stechen Messer*" (a stabbing knife) and Momma catches the blood in a big pan. She stirs the blood with her hand real fast, "so it won't clot," she says. The blood is later mixed with boiled meat parts from the butchered hog's head. All that is then stuffed inside the well-cleaned intestine of the same pig and boiled again outdoors in a big black cast-iron pot. It smells really good, but it is knowing what is in there. Blood! Phooey!

Farm children see a lot of stuff like that, and most don't think it's so bad. It just goes with living in the country. It is simply an accepted rule that nothing must ever go to waste! Some families make tamales instead of blood sausage. The same stuff goes into a tamale, except not the blood, I think!

I hate to watch any animal being killed for food. But I have been lectured too often. I am told I must understand that almost all our food has to come from our farm. And I admit, I love to eat ham and bacon and sausage . . . from that same hog. I just still can't stand eating blood sausage.

There's something else that appears on our breakfast table once a year at sausage-making time. That's scrambled eggs with brains

The early modern four-slice toaster for homemade bread. Wonderful for making toast over a hot bed of coals in a wood-burning stove. It was used by placing it over the smallest lid opening on the stovetop. If you forgot to turn the bread, well, "add it it to the hog slop or eat it anyway." Nothing must be thrown away.

— From the author's collection. Photo by Bill Nelson

and sweetbreads (the pancreas or the thymus gland from a calf). Of course, none of us kids will eat that! Momma and Daddy do and laugh at our delicate stomachs. We gladly let them have it all! We just eat our oatmeal—plain oatmeal: "*Danke! Das ist alles!*"

Sometimes we have eggs for breakfast. Momma fries them in that same big black skillet. As they get done, she places them on a large platter and they are kept in the warmer oven attached to and over our wood-burning stove. Sometimes the yolks get broken, sometimes not. The platter full of fourteen or more fried eggs always starts out with Daddy taking two or three eggs, and then the platter is passed around the table, with Momma being last. She does not seem to mind always being last.

Nobody ever complains about how the fried eggs are cooked. Everyone just takes what is there. Sometimes the eggs don't smell too good, but nobody says anything. We kids do glance at each other and frown. Finally, Momma says, "If I ever figure out which

Cast-iron frying pans were used to prepare every meal. The bottoms were never washed, as they were used over an open lid on the stove and were quite black with soot. The inside of the skillet was seldom washed, as they were cured with unsalted lard . . . unless gravy was cooked in it. Then it was washed but had to be re-larded. Messy job, that.

— From the Warren Hahn collection. Photo by Bill Nelson

hen lays those stinky eggs, we're going to have chicken and dumplings!" Days later, we'll have just that for dinner. The occasional smelly eggs never stop, though!

Today, after breakfast, Daddy read a letter to us from my sister, Bernice. They are living in Fort Worth, Texas where Art is working at a steel manufacturing company.

They found a furnished apartment for $37.50 a month. But they thought it was too expensive and found another one for $25 a month. They have to share the bathroom with another couple.

Momma's got big tears in her eyes and sadly shook her head. I think Momma misses Bernice as much as I do.

So, breakfast is over. Everybody goes off to work elsewhere, and it is my responsibility to wash all the dishes. I stand on a wooden box Daddy built just for me so I can reach the sink. I like standing on my special box. I don't like this chore.

First, I have to wait for the water to boil in the kettle on the stove. By the time that happens, the oatmeal or the eggs have dried on all the plates. Yes, we eat oatmeal off plates—never out of bowls. I don't know why!

Momma fixes a dishpan of warm water with some shaved homemade soap in it. She puts the pan in the sink and I begin to wash the dishes and rinse them in another pan of warm water she has prepared.

Warren is supposed to dry the dishes. He is standing on his own box to make him tall enough to reach the counter. Warren is shy and does not talk too much. But most of the time we giggle and sing funny songs like:

Sweet Ivory soap.
You are the dope.
You clean me so.
Like sopillo.

In all my dreams,
your fair face beams.
You are the apple of my eye.
Sweet Ivory Soap.

Arthur, Bernice's husband, taught us that song. I don't know where he learned it.

Anyway, just about the time we get through with the dishes, Momma brings in the cream separator. She tosses the used dishwater out of the back door—right over the heads of all our twenty cats. Every time the back door opens they all come running, thinking they are going to be fed some more. Sometimes Momma gets some of the cats wet. I think she does that on purpose. She laughs a lot when that happens!

Momma fixes another dishpan full of fresh hot water with homemade soap to wash the separator.

A cream separator is a mechanical device permanently attached to a sturdy table out in a corner of our screened-in porch. Atop that mechanical contraption is placed a round, heavy, steel, cone-shaped, spinning apparatus. On top of that fit two aluminum spouts (one on top of the other), and on top of them sits a large aluminum bowl which holds the freshly milked milk.

Daddy begins to turn the handle of the mechanical separator. He begins real slow, and a bell that's attached to the handle rings with every turn. As he turns faster and faster, the bell stops, Daddy opens the control valve to begin the separating process, the raw milk is spun through the separator, and just like magic, cream comes out of one spout and milk comes out of the other!

It's fun to watch the separator work even though we've seen it hundreds of times. The cream is much slower coming out of its spout than the milk. When it finally appears, Warren and I shout, "It's coming! Papa! It's a-coming! H-e-r-e comes the cream!"

Warren and I love to drink the foaming warm milk as it comes out of the spout, and we always giggle at each other's milk mustaches. Daddy laughs too and calls us giggle-boxes! Daddy runs the separator while breakfast is cooking on the stove.

But now it's time to wash this incredible separator, and that is not fun! There are so many parts! Inside the heavy cone-shaped piece of the separator are many, many smaller cones with holes all around them. Each cone has to be washed individually and then dried, of course. Warren does that, but it takes forever!

But if I complain, Momma reminds me how we are going to fix that pretty satin headboard. So, I do my work and daydream of the lovely bedroom I am going to have someday. I'll sleep like a log then.

While Warren and I are busy with the dishes, Momma starts the bread. She makes five loaves of bread every other day! There are six people to feed in our family, and three of them work outdoors. It seems like they are always hungry! Of course, Momma and I eat our share too. Freshly baked bread just out of the oven of a wood-burning stove is so delicious and too wonderful to describe!

Momma makes her own yeast cakes. One batch of bread takes

(Right): The cream separator was used every morning and was a vital part of farm life and living. Internet research shows that same centrifugal technology is still being used today—only electrified. (Left): A separator with parts shown to give understanding of how difficult it was to clean.

—From the Warren Hahn collection. Photos by Bill Nelson

one yeast cake. She drops one into a small bowl of warm water to dissolve. Then she puts a huge crockery pan on the small table in our kitchen. Into it she puts a little warm water, salt, sugar, and fresh lard, the dissolved yeast, and enough flour to make a sticky batter. She mixes all that together with a big steel spoon. Momma has used the spoon so much that it's worn off at one side and no longer looks like a normal spoon.

This sticky batter has to sit for a while to rise. When it is ready, Momma scatters a lot of flour on the table in our kitchen and then pours the sticky mess right on top of the flour. Then she begins to knead. She kneads it and kneads it with both hands, always adding a little bit of flour. After a while, Momma has flour up to her elbows and flour all over the front of her apron. Momma always wears an apron that has a bib that hangs around her neck and covers the front of her dress. The bib is sewn to a waist band that ties in back. Below the bib in front is the apron part, which covers the entire front of Momma's dress. Sometimes Warren and I pull the tie strings in back that loosen Momma's apron. She does not think that's as funny as we do.

"*Kinder, Kinder!* I think maybe you don't have enough work to keep you busy?"

Warren and I get pretty sober, pretty fast.

My next job every morning is to make up all the beds. I do complain about that often! I don't understand why my brothers can't make their own beds! Momma says that they have work to do. And I say, "So what am I doing—playing?"

Momma says sharply, "You're doing your share like everyone else, young lady."

I see the hurt look beginning in her eyes and I feel guilty.

"I know, Momma. I'm sorry. I just miss Bernice. Sometimes it just seems like since she's gone, our housework is never finished. I know Daddy and the boys work hard building fences and plowing fields and stuff like that. But they can at least see what they've done at the end of the day. We just cook, and everybody just gobbles it up and it's gone! Next day we start all over again!"

"*Ja, ja.* But working inside all day is important work, too. And it's hard, I know. But pretty soon we'll get to work on your headboard, and then we'll have some fun too!"

"I know, Momma. Maybe tomorrow we can begin?"

"We'll have to wait and see. So—*mach schnell, du kleine Puppe!* (Hurry up, you little doll!) We must start cooking dinner or we'll be late. I'll start the meat and you peel the potatoes. Then, while they're cooking, I'll brush your hair and plait it for you." I have long hair like my momma.

"Is it so bad working along the side of your momma?" I am sitting on the floor in front of Momma while she brushes my hair.

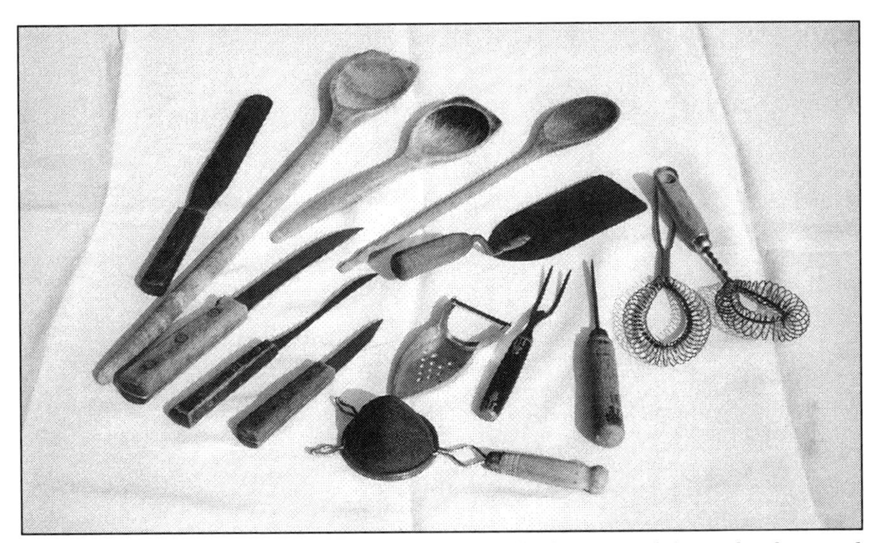

Everyday common cooking tools found in the 1930s kitchen. From left to right: thin metal cake icing spatula; long-handled wooden spoon used in cooking jams, jellies, and preserves; short wooden spoon to stir when cooking in enameled pots; a sharp butcher knife; the wood spoon used only for washing fresh butter; the thin-bladed paring knife for extra-thin peeling; thin tin spatula for turning eggs, pancakes, slipping cookies off cookie sheets, etc.; a short, stout paring knife for a small, firm vegetable such as potato, okra, green beans, onion, etc; a fine meshed strainer used for tea leaves and coffee grounds; a modern potato peeler—that never worked; a two-tined metal fork for frying bacon, ham, and steaks; the essential ice pick; and two wire whipping tools.

—From the Bill Nelson collection. Photo by Bill Nelson

"No, Momma. I am learning a lot of things about housework. You're a good teacher. So, tomorrow, Momma? Can we work on the headboard?"

"I told you, we have to wait and see. Be patient, *Puppe.* I want to begin the headboard as much as you do."

Momma is finished plaiting my hair, and she tugs both braids at the same time and then hugs my shoulders. "Now. We need to get a-hoppin'. Enough of this chatter!"

So that is the beginning of our day, every day—chores that must be done every morning. By midmorning the bread dough has risen enough for Momma to shape it into loaves and place them into bread pans. If we have enough time, Momma lets me take a glob of dough too and I work it and try to shape a loaf. She always shows Daddy the loaf I've shaped. I'm getting pretty good at it, I think. The pans of bread are now set inside the warmer bins attached to and extended over and above the wood stove. The loaves must now rise. They will be ready to bake around eleven o'clock and will be ready for our noon meal.

Next, there is cream to churn into butter. Momma puts the cream in a big heavy glass square jar and screws a metal lid on top. The lid has wooden paddles attached to its underside that go down into the cream. On top of the metal lid and attached to the wooden paddles are two little cog wheels with a small handle attached. I start cranking the handle round and round, turning fast while it is easy to turn. I turn it and turn it and turn it until finally the cream gets so stiff the paddles are hard to turn. Then Momma takes over and finishes turning until there is a glob of solid butter stuck on the paddles. What's left over in the bottom of the big glass jar now is called buttermilk.

Momma uses a wooden spoon and washes the butter several times in cold water. Then, she molds the butter into a dish. She lets me make a design on top of the butter with the wooden spoon. That's fun. Sometimes we use a pound-size wooden box to mold the butter. We don't do that often, as Momma sells our surplus cream to the creamery in Fredericksburg. We only keep enough cream for our family's butter.

After the butter is washed and molded into a dish we quickly set it inside the ice box to cool. Our ice box holds a large block of ice, and we must not hold the door open any longer than necessary. The ice melts quickly, and then we must drive seventeen miles to Fredericksburg to get more.

Sometimes we get ice from a truck that comes around our farm twice a week. It's fun to watch the ice man chip a small section off a huge block on the inside of his ice truck. Daddy says its a real trick to break off a perfect block of ice. He uses a huge ice pick to make a line of pick marks about a foot one way and then back to the edge.

Dazey Churn No. 40, patented 1922, St. Louis, Mo. This modern invention followed the old wooden-plunger type. Seeing cream turn into butter was always an exciting chore.

— From the Susan Kathryne Rose Durden collection. The churn was a gift from her mother, Dolly Kneupper Rose. It originally belonged to Dolly's mother, Mrs. Minnie Katherine Gourley Kneupper, from Kendalia, Texas. Photo by Bill Nelson.

Ice box. The upper unit contained the block of ice, which chilled the lower compartment. It was never to be held open longer than necessary and then was always, always be closed up and latched. Little fingers loved to seek out little pieces of loose chipped ice from the top compartment. Woe unto the one who was caught.

—From Antiquities, Etc., Comfort, Texas, Nancy Billingsley

Then he picks at it about a foot down the side and below where he wants the ice to break. Sure enough, a square block soon breaks off. He uses ice tongs to carry the dripping ice block inside our house and places it in the ice chamber. The ice is so clear it looks like glass. Once Warren and I yielded to temptation about that ice block. The weather was really hot, so we sneaked a little sliver of that ice out of the ice box. We forgot to latch the door! Oh, did Momma get angry when she discovered the melting block! And when Momma is angry, everybody hears about it. We won't do that again!

Our next chore is to help Momma make pie crusts. She has some flour left on the table from the bread mixing, and she rolls out the crust there with a rolling pin. I love to watch Momma when she picks up the crust, flips it, and places it in glass pie plates. It is my job to prick fork holes all over the bottom of the crusts.

Next we take the buttermilk, add sugar, beaten egg yolks, and Watkin's vanilla and we pour it into the pie shells. Buttermilk pie is my daddy's favorite. Some people like to drink buttermilk with sugar and vanilla added. But Momma says we stretch our buttermilk so that everybody can have some. Momma pops the pies into the oven. Later we will beat the egg whites to make meringue for the top of the pie.

Making meringue is very, very, very, very hard to do. I love to watch Momma beat egg whites. Momma has the egg whites in a medium-size glass bowl. She then takes a flat, paddle-like spoon made of coiled wires and she kind of tucks the bowl under her left side with her arm around the bowl. Then she beats the egg whites until they are frothy. She beats faster and faster until peaks form. Then she adds some sugar and beats and beats it again. I've tried it, and before I can even get the egg whites foamy, my arm feels like it will fall off. Momma says I need to get a little bigger first. Momma does it really good and the pies will be ready by lunchtime. Those pies will disappear in five minutes. It sure takes us a lot longer to make them.

Special baking tools for Momma's Christmas cookies.
—From the Bill Nelson collection. Photo by Bill Nelson

Next, we must work with clabbered milk (surplus milk that's been sitting at room temperature in a large bowl for a day or so and has soured and turned to clabber). Momma pours it into a clean, soft, often-washed, empty cloth sugar sack. She ties a knot at the top, then hangs the dripping sack outside on the wash line with clothes pins. It will hang outside all day to drain off the whey. The whey goes into the slop bucket for the hogs.

By the end of the day the clabber in the sack will be drained out, and now it is *Schmier Käse* (cream cheese). We'll have it for the evening meal, called supper. Along with the *Schmier Käse* we'll have cornbread, fresh butter, sometimes sausage, other times with onion slices and tomatoes. Sometimes we have *Schmier Käse* with molasses.

Sometimes the *Schmier Käse* is left to hang outside for several days instead of several hours. It hangs until it is very, very dry. Momma then takes the sack and empties the hard clump of what Momma now calls *Krümel Käse* into a bowl. With her hands she crumbles it into small, fine pieces. She then ties a soft, clean dish towel over the bowl and sets it aside in a dark kitchen closet for a day or so or until it "smells just right." I don't know why they say it smells just right, because what it does is stink like spoiled rotten stuff! But when Momma puts that "stuff" in her black cast-iron frying pan and cooks it over the wood-burning stove, my daddy almost has fits to hurry up and eat it! He calls it *Koch Käse*. Serve it to Daddy with homemade bread and butter and honey and Daddy always hugs Momma big-time when she has fixed *Koch Käse* for supper!

But back to the schmier kasse and cornbread and molasses. Having good molasses for the table is every farmer's delight. For me too, because that is the one and only time I am allowed to go out in the field to work.

The making of molasses is a family project—except Momma. She stays home and does her work alone today. Molasses-making day begins just at daylight. It's time to strip off all the leaves of the sugar cane Daddy has planted and grown in the field.

The stalks are almost twelve to fourteen inches taller than Warren and I can reach. But we begin at the bottom to pull off all the leaves right up to the head of grain. Daddy and my brothers then come along behind us, finish pulling off the remaining leaves, and then cut off all the heads. Some of those heads of grain will be dried and stored for seed for next year's crop of sugar cane. The rest will be used to feed our chickens and livestock.

Next, the now bare, stripped stalks of cane are cut off at ground level and tied into bundles. Daddy and my brothers then pile all the bundles onto the wagon and they get hauled to Fredericksburg,

Wood cook stove with warmer at top.

— From the Durden Ranch Home at Doss and now in the Susan Rose Durden collection. Photo by Bill Nelson

where there's a molasses press. We kids all pile onto the wagon. We get to ride along!

By the time we go the seventeen miles to Fredericksburg and Mr. Schmidtzensky's place, there is one other wagon ahead of us also loaded with bundles of cane. We unload our bundled stalks and pile them all in the spot that Mr. Schmidtzensky has pointed out for us. Our load will be the second one to be pressed. That means our stalks of cane will be fed into a huge, wringer-like press that is being turned by two horses that are tethered to a long pole. They walk round and round and turn the big rollers on the press. The green-colored juices in the stalks are squeezed out into large containers. That sweet juice is then taken to a nearby shed where there's a vat with a hot wood fire underneath. The juice is poured into that vat and boiled and boiled while Mrs. Schmidtzensky uses a huge, long wooden paddle to stir the juice until it turns into molasses syrup.

Daddy has brought along two five-gallon tin cans. When our molasses is done, Mrs. Schmidtzensky uses a big dipper with a long handle to pour the thick syrup into our cans. We have to wait for it to cool a little before we can put the lid on it.

Daddy says it's a special talent to cook good molasses. If it is cooked too long, the syrup turns into sugar. If it is not cooked long enough, it turns sour. There are several molasses presses that have had to close because they didn't have the "molasses cooking know-how."

The Schmidtzenskys are an old, trusted molasses-making family. Daddy pays him and shakes his hand. I like to watch my daddy shake hands with someone he admires and respects. There is a special look that is exchanged between grown-ups when they appreciate each other. Mr. Schmidtzensky wears a big, wide-brimmed hat, and he smiles broadly and nods his head repeatedly while my daddy is shaking his hand and bidding him goodbye.

The making of our ten gallons of molasses has taken all day, and it's nightfall by the time we return home. But we have enough molasses now to last us until next year's crop of sugar cane. It is a source of great pride to have sweet molasses in the cellar come wintertime. Daddy also loves Momma's molasses cookies!

As Momma and I set about our work, I daydream a lot about the blue satin headboard for my bedroom. I try to get Momma to talk about it as often as I can. Momma keeps using the word "patience." "*Du must Geduld haben.*" (You must have patience.) I don't like that word, Geduld.

But *patience* sounds a little like *princess*. I wonder if a princess would have to wash a separator—or make up beds—or strip sugar cane? Oh, well! Momma says we all have to work together because we are a family. I do love my family. "*Ja,* Momma. Patience!"

Chapter Four

Blue Satin Soothes the Soul

After Momma said we could turn my bed's headboard into a satin padded one, I spent a lot of time at night, when I'm trying to go to sleep alone now, imagining how that would be done. My bed is a simple one—like most farm beds I've seen. My full-bed-size headboard is not a board at all. It is actually made of a hollow steel tube—about three inches in diameter. The tube starts at the floor, where it has a roller fixed to it. The tube then comes straight up about thirty inches above the springs and mattress; then, with a gentle curve crosses the width of the bed and with the same gentle curve it goes downward and continues all the way to the floor, where there is another roller.

Inside this frame are several smaller vertical tubes that are stuck into the three-inch tube at the inside top and end up stuck into another small tube running straight across from left to right at the spring and mattress level. You could almost describe the head of my bed as a huge comb for a giant! Don't think about it that way, I tell myself!

Typical farm bed showing the headboard that becomes the saving grace for the little girl who became the author of this book.

— From the restored farm home at Jingle Beall Farm in Comfort, Texas. From the Susan Rose Durden collection. Photo by Bill Nelson

While my momma and I work together during the day, we talk a lot about how we will pad the headboard. She says we will pack cotton between those upright tubes and then hold it in place by quilting it onto old quilts. Then, we will sew up an old sheet to fit over the whole headboard—sort of like a huge pillowcase. Next, we'll use a long, ten-inch curved needle that Daddy uses to sew up his wool sacks at shearing time. We'll stick that needle back and forth through all the padding until we are sure it will all stay in place.

The more we talk about the project, the more impatient I become. I think Momma is getting that way too. Momma actually bought the light blue satin material a week ago in Fredericksburg! She asked, "Would you like to keep it in your room?"

I did! Momma does not know it, but I keep it beside me in my bed at night! First thing in the morning, I return it to my closet.

Sometimes, I get it out when Momma and I sit on my bed as we plan our project. The exquisite heavy blue satin material is so grand

and shiny! We both place our hands on it, and while we are talking we caress it lightly and lovingly as if it was a precious and blessed treasure. For me it truly is! For Momma it probably means a good night's sleep!

"Maybe," Momma says softly with hope in her voice, "maybe we can begin this project on Monday—after we've done the wash."

Chapter Five

Monday's Backache Blues

I have a difficult time getting out of bed on Monday. The day begins so very, very early—even before daylight, because it's *Waschtag* (laundry day). In addition to all our usual breakfast chores and washing the dishes, Oliver and I go out to our wash house to start a fire under the huge copper kettle. We are to fill it with rainwater.

The rainwater comes from a huge rainwater tank that Daddy built atop a low cement foundation in our back yard just outside, but attached to, our washhouse. The wash house is actually only one room which adjoins the smoke house and also Daddy's workshop/tank house. All those rooms are under one roof and guttered in such a way that all our rainfall is collected and flows into our rainwater tank. This water is precious and is used only for washing clothes and our hair. It is considered soft water and very desirable for those two purposes.

We are better off than most farms, as Daddy is a problem-solver and an innovator. He is always coming up with a plan to make our work easier. Like, for instance, he built inside one corner of our

The Hahns' rainwater tank and the door into the wash house.
— Photo taken at the Warren and Katie Hahn home in Doss, Texas. Also childhood home of Nancy Clara (Hahn) Ippolito, to whom this book is dedicated. Photo by Bill Nelson.

wood-framed wash house a large concrete block which holds that copper kettle. The cement block/oven has a red brick chimney attached and goes up outside the wall to carry the smoke away. While most farms have a wash house, it is typical to have a black kettle to heat water for washing located outside, somewhere near-by. There, the kettle hangs on an iron frame and water has to be carried a longer distance both ways. So, our special water heating/cement block/oven, right inside our wash house, is considered a great luxury and convenience. It also keeps our washhouse warm in winter.

So, on Monday, Oliver and I carry bucket after bucket of rain-water and empty them into that huge copper kettle until it is full. The buckets of water are heavy, and because I am just a little girl, I fill mine only part way. I notice the kettle is not filling very fast. So I find a second bucket to set under the rainwater faucet to fill while I am carrying the other to empty. I have to run to keep up! I don't

The ruler is to show the depth of the enormous copper kettle.
— From the Warren Hahn collection. Photo by Bill Nelson

dare let the bucket run over. Momma would scold me for that! So I run and run, back and forth. I wonder why it always seems to take Oliver such a long time to build the fire under the kettle. He always seems to get through right after I have the kettle filled! Oliver is a prankster. Sometimes he makes me pretty angry!

Once the kettle is full, wood is constantly stoked and burned under the copper bucket until the water is steaming and boiling hot. My brothers, before they leave for the field this morning, chop and carry a pile of wood into the wash house and also chopped split wood into our kitchen.

While the water is heating in the wash house, back inside our house, Momma and I are busy doing all the usual morning chores.

We also start the noon meal either baking or cooking in or on the stove while we do the wash (laundry). That means, of course, that we have to make many trips back and forth between the wash house and the main house to keep both wood fires burning. I sing softly to myself, "I'm going to get a headboard, a headboard, a pretty satin headboard—and I will be a princess, a princess—"

Momma and I strip off all the bed sheets and gather all the dirty laundry in a big pile on the back screened-in porch. Momma and I then sort it into, not only colors, but also into dirty and dirtiest!

"Oh, Momma! Daddy's coveralls stink just like an old billy goat! Phew!" I hold my nose as I toss it on the dirtiest pile.

"Ja! Ja! Das riecht nicht gut!" (Yes! Yes! I know that smell is not good!)

Let me tell you true! With sweating men laboring and plowing in fields and working with cattle and sheep and goats—especially billy goats—or rounding up on horseback—none of their dirty work clothes smells great!

The really nice clothes my family owns are worn only to church on Sunday or on special occasions. There are not many of that kind. All our clothes are made of cotton. Our good clothes have to be washed by hand on a scrub board, rinsed carefully, then starched and ironed to look nice and neat. Momma is clear about that! Momma is a stickler for never wearing any good clothes that are not ironed. Ironing happens on Tuesday.

The water is boiling now, and we begin the machine washing around eight o'clock. The water has to be lifted bucket by bucket out of the copper kettle and poured into the washing machine. Momma does that. Next, a block of homemade soap is dropped into the hot water and the agitator set in motion.

The washing machine is set in motion by a belt and a gasoline engine my father has rigged up at the side of the washing machine. It is another one of my daddy's innovations. He warned all of us that it's very dangerous to be at the belt side, as sometimes the belt slips off the pulley and is quite capable of slapping you and wounding the person standing nearby. My oldest brother found that out the hard way one day. He had started the motor for us and was just stepping away when the belt slipped off its pulley. It knocked him to the cement floor. We stood there speechless until Momma cried out, "*Gott im Himmel!* Are you all right?"

Otto Junior picked himself up off the hard cement floor. After it was determined there were no broken bones, we younger kids were reminded again how dangerous it is to stand anywhere near the belt while it is going!

Before we started using this gasoline engine, Daddy backed up our Model T Ford to the north window of our wash house. He'd jack up the rear wheel, removed the tire and used our Model T Ford rear wheel hub as a pulley. The belt came in through the low window and was attached to the washing machine pulley. That was not too successful.

After that came the purchase of a John Deere tractor. It came with a fly wheel attached to the front. We used it to operate the washing machine for a while. The John Deere tractor was called a "Poppin' Johnny," and that was absolutely correct. The gasoline motor driving the washing machine was noisy too, but not like that tractor!

But back to our wash. Our white clothes are the first load to be washed: That's Daddy's and my three brothers' white Sunday shirts, white handkerchiefs, homemade cotton slips, homemade cotton men's underwear, and Momma's crocheted doilies and embroidered pillow slips. Momma also has a beautiful white damask tablecloth that is washed whenever we've had dinner guests on Sunday. This special tablecloth and napkins are heirlooms from her mother, Grandma Lange. They are very pretty and must have very special starch and special ironing.

Before the first clothes go into the washing machine, they are soaked in a cold-water tub. Then, they are put through a wringer which is simply two white rubber rollers with an attached handle turned by hand. The clothes come out of the wringer and go down

Another unpleasant memory: the washtub, the scrub board, and the scrub brush bring back remembrances of skinned knuckles and rough, red, chapped hands.

— From North Creek Antiques, 509 9th Street, Comfort, Texas, Beth Richardson, collector. Photo by Bill Nelson

into the hot, sudsy water. We put the lid back on the washtub and set the agitator in motion by moving a handle forward.

After about fifteen minutes, depending on how dirty the load is, Momma turns off the agitator and lifts the clothes out of the hot suds with a wash stick—an old ax handle my daddy has shortened for her. Momma lifts the clothes with one hand and then works them again into the wringer with the other hand. They feed down into the first rinse-water tub. Sometimes I have to use both hands to start to turn the wringer for Momma.

After we have taken that first load out of the hot, sudsy water, a second load—which has been soaking—is put through the wringer and feeds down into the suds for load number two. It will wash while we continue to work with the first load.

The first load is now swished back and forth to rinse and then fed through the wringer, where it goes into a third tub of rinse water. Momma can turn the wringer herself now, since she can rinse the clothes out of the cool rinse water with one hand and turn the wringer with the other.

This third tub has wash blue in the water. It is supposed to make white clothes look whiter. If you put in too much, it makes your white clothes look blue!

Next the load is put through the wringer once again and dropped into some hot Argo starch Momma has mixed with hot in a bucket. Once more, it's back through the wringer for the final time.

Momma and I can now carry that load of clothes out to the wash lines. I hand the wet clothes to Momma—one piece at a time—and she hangs up the clothes to dry. They are pinned onto the wire with wooden spring-type clothes pins. It is my job to hand Momma the clothes pins too. Sometimes my minds wanders, or I am busy talking, and I forget that part of my job. When I do that, Momma says, "*Puppe!* Pay attention to your work!" I'm sorry I'm not tall enough to reach the lines yet. I find my job kind of dull!

Having completed that job, Momma and I go back to get the next load that's been washing while we were hanging up the previous load. We usually have at least six loads to wash.

By noon all our lines are filled. Daddy's and my brother's overalls are hanging over the yard fence to dry. We are relieved to know the lines are not overloaded or that they might break—again! That happened to us not long ago, and Momma cried and cried. That's when Daddy built new wash lines. We now have six new twenty-foot-long wash lines with support poles in the middle of those twenty feet of wire. We have also learned to hang the heavy clothes near the support poles and balance the weight on the lines! Daddy and Momma had a few words about that!

Momma and I are very proud when we have all our lines filled with sparkling-clean laundry hanging out and waving in the sun.

We are thankful it is not a cloudy or damp day. Today our clothes will dry quickly.

Momma and I congratulate ourselves. We have finished our wash, we will have dinner on the table by twelve o'clock noon, and Momma has the bread dough ready to put into pans to rise. It will be late baking today.

Momma and I are a good team. Constructing a satin-covered, padded headboard should be no problem for us—if we can ever get started!

"Be patient," Momma reminds me. "*Geduld!*" I like that word less every time I hear it.

Meanwhile, back to the laundry! The three washtubs and the washing machine now need to be emptied. Since we've completed our project by dinnertime, today my brothers and Daddy simply lift the tubs by their handles and carry the water out to the flowers or garden. Had the timing not worked out so well, I would have had to carry the water out—bucket by bucket.

Momma also says the soapy water left in the washing machine is too dirty today to be used to scrub the floor of our screened porch. I smile to myself when Momma says that. I hum and sing to the tune of "Baa, Baa, Black Sheep":

Blue satin,
Lovely satin,
Waiting in a box.
Soon you'll be a headboard
For little Goldilocks!

After our noon meal, Momma and I bring in the clothes that are dry and pile them all on Momma's bed. It is one big pile! I neatly fold all the towels, red and blue work handkerchiefs, dishtowels, and underwear. Momma folds the work pants and shirts. Clothes to be ironed are put in a separate pile. Momma will sprinkle those with water later, and wrap them in an old worn-out bedsheet, where they will wait to be ironed tomorrow—Tuesday.

Momma and I then return all the nice and clean sheets to the beds. Clean sheets, dried in the sun, always smell special. We have only five good sheets. My brothers all sleep on single beds, and their sheets are usually the ones that wear out first. Momma always scolds them when she hears horsing around in their room. I think it's the sheets she is worried about. They are very expensive! I'm glad there are some torn sheets! They are going to be used for my headboard someday—maybe.

Not today, though. I can understand that. It is getting dark, and Momma and I are very tired. Everybody is tired. After supper, my weary family sits out on the front porch and we talk for a while. After that, I am content just to go to bed and rest.

I fall asleep and dream. There is a huge bed with a blue satin padded headboard in my bedroom. My bed is so big it fills the entire room! It is so tall I must climb up into it with a ladder. My gown is like the headboard—made of blue satin. I am a princess. I climb and climb and climb. I never seem to be able to get all the way up and into the bed.

Chapter Six

The Beginning

Tuesday is not so frantic as Monday. The clothes sprinkled down last night are ready, and Momma begins ironing early. She switches off between four heavy black irons that are heated on the wood stove.

Warren and I get the morning dishes and separator washed and the beds made and the kitchen swept out. Next, I relieve Momma so she can start the bread. I stand on my dishwashing box and iron the white handkerchiefs. I also iron the small embroidered pillow slips that have been heavily starched. If I don't get them as smooth as Momma wants them, she will re-sprinkle and re-iron them herself. I want to help Momma really good today and maybe, maybe we can get to my headboard. Momma hinted earlier that we just might begin our project this afternoon! I work as hard and as fast as I am able—even though the iron is almost too heavy for me. I know the bread is set and dinner is getting done too. I truly expect that today may be the day! My heart begins to sing.

While I iron, Momma opens her Sears and Roebuck treadle sewing machine and mends Daddy's and my brother's clothes. If

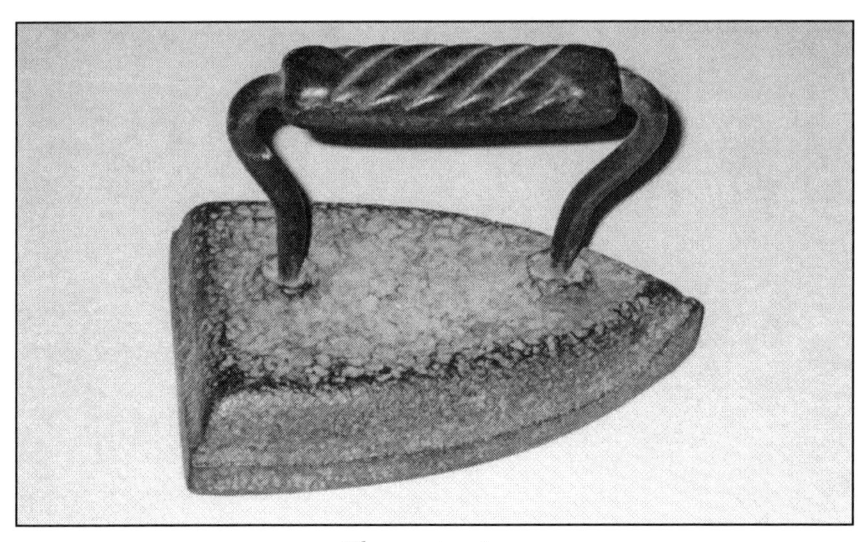

The cast-iron iron.
— From the Warren Hahn collection. Photo by Bill Nelson

something is so torn that it can't be mended, it is saved for patchwork material or quilt pieces. If it's too torn to be reused in any other way, Momma gives it to our cats for a bed. Nothing is ever thrown away.

Momma has left the socks with holes for us to darn sometime during the week. Momma has also left the sewing machine open! That is a good sign. Maybe she plans to use it later—on my headboard making!

After lunch, we finish with the ironing and mending, and while I am doing the dinner dishes, I hear Momma rummaging around in the next room.

"Momma? What are you doing?"

"I'm getting some stuff together."

"For my headboard, Momma?"

"Ja. Das ist richtig."

"Don't start without me, Momma!"

"I won't. *Mach schnell!*" (Hurry up!)

Our project is to begin! I know we will be done with it by nighttime. I am so excited I can hardly breathe. I put some of the dishes away a little wet—let the air dry them today!

Momma and I put my tubular headboard on an old quilt and sheet that we have spread out on the floor in the living room. Daddy had taken the headboard off my bed several days ago. My bed springs and mattress are temporarily propped up on wooden boxes.

Momma and I sit on the floor. Momma instructs me to pull out of a sack all the cotton she has left over from past quilting projects. She shows me how to lay it between the upright tubes of the headboard. It didn't take long for me to realize that we didn't have near-

Inside this cabinet is the treadle sewing machine from Sears and Roebuck which was Momma's birthday gift when she turned sixteen years old (March 1911).

— From the author's collection. Photo by Bill Nelson

ly enough padding! My throat feels tight and I am on the verge of tears. Momma sees my lips quiver and my voice is weak. "Momma, what are we going to do now?"

"*Du mußt nicht weinen!* (You must not cry.) This is not a problem we can't solve. You know that bunch of old rags and material scraps in the window-seat storage in the boys' room?"

"*Ja,* Momma."

"Let's go dig around and let's see what we can find in there. It doesn't matter what we use for padding. It won't show, and no one will ever know. We could even use some dried corn shucks if we have to. Did you know that the Indians and even your own great-grandparents used to sleep on mattresses filled with corn shucks?"

I looked at my momma's face. "You're so smart, Momma."

"*Ja!*" She laughs and tweaks my nose as we both jump up from the floor. "And don't you forget it!"

Momma and I find lots and lots of fabric scraps and old socks and even pieces of old soft blankets in the window seat. We go through the entire contents stored in there and stuff it all into a sack. Momma and I are laughing as we agree that we will have enough padding now!

We did not completely empty out the window-seat fabric scraps because when it's "kidding time" for our goats we will need some of these scraps. They will be used like this: We tear two strips off the same material and tie one piece around the momma goat's leg and the other, matching piece around her baby kid's leg. That way if the momma, the nanny, does not accept her baby, Daddy and the boys will put her baby with her and tie the momma to a post to allow her baby to nurse. Otherwise we will have to bottle feed the baby goat, and no farmer likes to do that.

One time, we did have a lot of baby goats to bottle. I was helping Oliver bottle feed them. I was wearing a new dress Momma had made for me—one that had a buttoned-up front. Well, before I realized it, one of those sorry little goat kids was chewing on the material of the hem on the bottom of my new dress and had succeeded in biting a piece out of it! Boy, oh, boy! Did Momma scold me for not remembering to change into something old before I went to help Oliver. And, of course, Oliver did not remind me to do that either. I guess I need to be fair about it. I should have remembered but—I just get so excited around those cute and funny little goat kids.

"Oh, well. Nobody's perfect," Momma said after she cooled off. That incident was the topic of our family session out on the front porch that night. Everybody laughed about it—so I finally laughed too. Later Momma sewed a patch to replace the chewed-off piece and made me wear it for everyday work clothes. Nobody wears patched clothes on Sunday!

But, back to our headboard project!

Momma and I drag the heavy sack of "stuffing" into the living room and continue placing the material scraps between the uprights on my headboard.

Momma said, "I will buy a new bolt of cotton my next trip into Fredericksburg. The final layer must be smooth new cotton. If we're going to fix you a fancy bed, young lady, it must be a dandy! I just hope our hens lay lots of eggs between now and my next trip to Fredericksburg."

I hugged her. "*Danke schön, danke schön,* Momma."

"*Du bist meine kleine Puppe. Nicht wahr?*" (You are my little doll. Isn't that right?)

"No, Momma. *Ich bin eine grosse Puppe!*" (I am a big doll.)

Later that afternoon, Momma said we had to quit working on the headboard.

"It is time to go to the garden to pick our string beans, cucumbers, tomatoes, and okra. We will leave our unfinished headboard project on the living room floor. We must have *Geduld.*"

Later, when I saw everything we had harvested, I knew tomorrow was going to be another busy work day. There would be no time for my headboard. But, that's okay. We have made a good beginning today. I will practice patience like Momma said.

Chapter Seven

Canning Centipedes

Early Wednesday morning, Momma asked Warren and me to bring the canning jars out from under the house where they are stored when they're emptied during the year. It is a scary and dark, adventurous assignment. Warren wanted to crawl farther into the black spaces under our house, he said.

But I said, "Remember last year? We found a centipede in a jar—it was as long as the quart jar that it was in!"

Warren didn't crawl another inch. I smiled to myself.

We loaded our big red wagon full of jars and carefully took them to the back door. I pulled the wagon and Warren pushed. We have a nice sidewalk around this north side of our house. Daddy and the boys built it.

Our house is only two years old. My momma's brother, Uncle Arnold Lange, a carpenter, built if for my family during the Depression. Momma said not many people had enough money to build houses at that time, and that is why Uncle Arnold was unemployed and happy to come out to our place to work. He and Daddy

The original house, as it came with the purchase of the Hahn farm in 1918 at Doss, Texas.
— From the Warren Hahn collection

The new house, built in 1936, a difficult period of the Depression for the Hahn family. The front porch became a general meeting place for the family.
— From the Warren Hahn collection

tore down the old house that was on the farm when it was purchased. With that used lumber and a little new, they built and painted the new house. Uncle Arnold laughs a lot and has a big, bushy mustache. I like it when he calls me *"Die Lorichen."*

When Warren and I get to the back door with the jars, Momma shows us where to unload them by the door of the back porch. "Be very careful. Don't break any jars." Momma will take them into the kitchen as needed.

We go back for another load, and this time Warren gets to ride in the wagon. I pull him extra fast and the wagon bumps over the flat rocks Daddy and the boys have cemented together for our sidewalk. We laugh and giggle so much we throw ourselves on the soft ground beside our sidewalk. We roll and tumble as we do so. Finally, we hear Momma at the open window of the dining room. *"Kinder, Kinder, mach schnell!"*

When we are through hauling jars, Momma has stoked lots of split wood into the firebox of our stove to get water boiling. Warren and I are standing at the sink once again on our special wooden boxes in the kitchen. Momma pours the boiling water over the washed jars for us. We, Warren and I, have to step off and back away during this process. It is dangerous work with that boiling water and jars. But it is important that the jars be sterilized. Centipedes, you know!

Warren and I both dry the jars after they have drained and cooled a bit. We line them up on a clean towel on the small table in the kitchen and drape a clean towel over them to keep them sterile.

Warren is asked to bring more wood from the wood pile. He will use the wagon. Meanwhile, Momma shows me how to wash the green beans, string them, and pack them into jars. It's neat to see those long green string beans standing up in the glass jars. Momma then says I should put one teaspoon of canning salt on top of each jar of green beans. Next, Momma pours boiling water over the beans, fills the jar to the top, and then seals each jar with special lids and rings.

Our canner has room for seven quart jars. Momma sets the canner on top of the stove and places the jars filled with beans inside. She then put lots more wood in the fire box for high heat. When the water in the bottom of the canner begins to boil, she places the heavy lid on the canner and screws the clamps very tight.

Now we must wait for the steam to whistle out of the pepcock. When we hear that, Momma slips her hand inside a heavy mitten potholder and flips the steaming pepcock shut. Now we must wait

The pressure canner used by all housewives during the Depression years of the 1930s.

— From the Guernsey Museum, Guernsey, Wyoming. Permission Diane Griffith, Guernsey, Wyoming. Photo by Bill Nelson

once again for the pressure inside the canner to push the pressure gauge up to the specified point for preserving green beans. "Fifteen pounds of pressure for fifteen minutes," Momma reads from her Ball canning book.

Then comes the trick that spells success or failure for our canning. The pressure inside the canner must be maintained exactly for a specified amount of time. That means more wood in the stove—not too much and not too little. This part of the canning process always makes Momma nervous. Me too! If the pressure is too high, the jars will break. If it is not high enough, the beans will spoil.

While Momma is tending to the canner, I begin to wash okra pods and cut them in one-inch pieces for gumbo. Okra gets really slimy in water. Warren and I have fun playing with the slimy strings—until Momma tells us to stop.

The canner has been at the pressure level long enough now, and Momma tells us to stand back as she lifts the heavy canner off the stove and sets it on the table, where there is a slab of wood for it to sit on. Momma again puts on the heavy quilted mitten and opens the pepcock. Steam rushes out and makes a whistling sound.

When all the pressure is gone and the gauge is back to zero, Momma unscrews the heavy metal latches and slowly lifts the canner lid off with great caution. She says that sometimes a bad jar could blow up. I have never seen it happen. I wonder. Would we have green beans all over our ceiling in the kitchen if one blew up?

Momma will let the jars cool a bit before she transfers the wet, bright green, bean-filled jars out of the canner, dries them off, and sets them in the corner of the table to cool. When Daddy and my brothers come home, they will carry them into the cellar, where they are stored for winter use. Some of our best-looking jars of vegetables are saved to take to our community fair in Doss in August. We have won several blue ribbons!

Momma now takes the okra I have cut for gumbo and brings it to a boil in a big open pot. I wash and cut up onions for her to add to the pot too.

"I don't like cutting up onions, Momma. They burn my eyes and make me cry."

"*Ja, ja,*" she laughs and imitates crying. "*Was soll ich tun? Eilig, eilig!*" (Yes, yes. What can I do about that? Hurry. Hurry.)

Next, while the okra and onions are simmering, Momma pours boiling water over a large metal pan full of ripe tomatoes. I quickly fish them out with a slotted spoon and drain them on a soft cloth. The skins come off easily now. Momma chops them into the gumbo as fast as I can skin them for her.

I move on to our next vegetables that have been chilling in a pan with cracked ice. I wash, dry, and pack small to medium cucumbers into pint jars to make pickles. Momma then sends me out to the garden with small garden shears to cut fresh dill. It will be washed and stuffed into the bottom of the jars before I pack in the cucumbers. Momma is boiling some vinegar, water, and salt. She will pour that brine over the cucumbers and the dill and seal the jars. In fourteen days we'll have fresh, crisp dill pickles!

Outside, walking to the garden, the cool fresh air feels wonderful on my face! I want to stay outside and play. I stop and pet our three new kittens. Baby animals are a part of farm life I love. There's always some new baby animal born around her. My favorite are baby piggies. They are so funny to watch.

I laugh at the kittens rolling and tumbling around. I take a deep breath. I wish I could stay here. But I know if we are ever going to get through with all the canning, I had better forget playing. I also better remember to wash my hands when I get back inside the house! Momma is very particular about clean hands around food! Soiled hands will make spoiled canning.

I cut the dill. I like the smell of fresh dill. Oh, yuck! My hands still smell like onions!

While I am walking back to the house, I am thinking of what we have still to do today. The rest of the tomatoes, for sure. That's easy. Momma will pour boiling water over them, and I'll skin them and she will pack them into jars. To can tomatoes, Momma will again use the pressure canner.

Momma and I also are cooking catsup, tomato sauce, and on and on it goes.

"Our cellar will be full after this summer's harvest," Momma says proudly.

I am just a little girl, but I know that's important. Almost everything we eat comes from our farm. Meat, vegetables, fruit, eggs, milk, and more.

When I return from the garden with the dill, I wash my hands with soap in the bathroom. I dawdle a bit, not anxious to get back to the kitchen. The heat from the wood burning stove is smothering and stifling. Momma's face glistens with perspiration, and she stops often to wipe her face with her apron. Several times I hear her sigh with fatigue.

We work on and on and on until very late in the afternoon. In the meantime, Momma and I talk about church and how school will be beginning for me in September!

"It will be such fun when you start school! I always liked going to school." Momma spoke with enthusiasm of happy things to come for me. Momma adds, with sad look on her face, "I wish I'd had more schooling. Daddy and I only went to the eighth grade, you know. Eight grades was all there was to school back when we were children. We were so proud to learn to read and write and do numbers. Your daddy was really good at doing numbers."

Momma smiles. "I'm so glad we have a good school in Doss now. You will be a good student. I believe boys and girls should get a good education. I wish I would have—"

Momma rambles on and on. I don't listen too carefully, thinking that the olden days sure were not much fun. I was glad I didn't live back then.

I could tell from Momma's voice that she was very tired. She was trying hard not to be too discouraging about all the hard work that goes with being a farmer's wife. But she hints that girls should not be too quick to marry farmers.

A picture relating to Momma's school days, 1904. Momma is sixth from the left.
— From the author's collection

That night, in bed, I think about some of the things Momma said. I think I am beginning to dislike living on a farm! The work never ends! I also wish I had been born a boy. Maybe outdoors there is more freedom and, even better, fresh air! And fun! Daddy and the boys are always laughing about stuff that happens during the day.

Being a girl is different, Momma says. Momma sounded so serious and sometimes almost sad—like today—about always having to work so hard. Someday soon, she said, maybe things will be better and easier.

I fell into a troubled sleep.

In my sleep I continued to fill jar after jar after jar of something. I woke up with a gasp when I recognized—I was canning centipedes!

I wake up scared! I want to scream out for Momma! Maybe there is a centipede in my bed! I am petrified. I cautiously moved my feet around a little. I whimper and I am about to cry out for Momma when I remember how tired she looked at the end of today. I did not call out to her then. I did cry a little bit but I didn't make a sound. I must be a big girl, I told myself. Hanging on real tight to the blue satin material in bed next to me, I whisper to myself. "Soon I am going to go to school—to school! I am going to learn to read and write and do numbers." I wonder what one does with numbers—it sure didn't add up to me, didn't make any sense at all. Oh, well, if my daddy was good at numbers, he could tell me what it is. I must remember to ask him at breakfast.

Next thing I knew it was daylight. Momma must have let me sleep late! I can hear my family laughing. Yuck! I'll probably have to sit in the middle of our bench today. Oh, well. Here I go.

Chapter Eight

On Making Progress

As summer flies by, we occasionally find time to work on my headboard, but for only short periods of time. Our plan of action is going well—it is just too slow.

When we have all the padding laid in place, Momma and I begin to sew by hand with Daddy's big wool sack needle. I sit on one side of the headboard holding it upright and Momma is on the other. I poke the needle through the padding, and as soon as Momma can get a hold of the needle with a pair of pliers, she pulls it through. Then, she pokes from her side and I pull with the pliers.

It takes lots and lots of string. Sometimes we take the string over the top of the headboard to hold the padding in place so it can't slip down. It is very difficult to poke the heavy needle through all that padding, and our arms get tired.

But, even so, I'm growing more and more excited as the headboard begins to take shape. I am beginning to believe that it really is going to happen just like Momma promised it would.

But I'm beginning to worry a little. It is almost August, and school will begin for me in September. Then Momma will have to do all the housework alone. I begin to feel anxious again, and sometimes my bedroom seems a long, long way away from my momma. Sometimes I can hardly keep from crying at night when I am in my bed, so tired and all alone, and everything is so dark. I wish my sister would come home. Momma tells me she is living in California now and it's far away. Her husband has joined the Navy and they are stationed in a place called San Diego. They write letters often saying they're coming home for Christmas. Oh, I hope my headboard will be finished by then. Bernice will be amazed how I have "fixed up" our room! Momma and I have not told her about it in our letters. We want her to be surprised.

"Momma?" I call out from my room after we have all gone to bed. "What happens when I go to school? Will my headboard ever get finished?"

Momma sounded tired when she called back from their bedroom down the hallway, "*Puppe!* I promised you, didn't I? We'll get it done by Christmas—maybe even before! First we have to get you into school. *Nicht wahr?* (Isn't that right?)"

"*Ja,* Momma. I will like that."

Momma came to sit on the side of my bed for a while. She pulled the covers up to my chin to tuck me in. Momma is smiling as she smoothes back my hair. "*Schlaff gut, meine schöne kleine Puppe.*" (Sleep well, my pretty little doll.)

"Thank you, Momma. You *schlaff gut,* too."

Chapter Nine

A Mystery Is Solved

It was near to the end of summer. Daddy and my brothers worked long, hard hours harvesting the crops from the field. Momma and I have to stop our work every morning around ten o'clock to fix a midmorning snack to take out to them. Today we've made sandwiches on homemade bread slices, of course. We cut the meat off the soup bones and ground it up with onion and pickles. We've also packed coffee, iced tea, and some of Momma's molasses cookies into a basket and, carrying the heavy load of food, Momma and I trudge out to where they are.

Our huge field is in front of our house, and we can always see where they are because our house is built on the side of a typical Texas Hill Country hill. From the back yard you see a gentle slope that goes to the top of the hill. Our entire yard has been filled in with dirt so our yard is level. In the front of our house there are eight steps to climb to get up to our house and yard. It is one of the most beautiful vistas in the Hill Country.

I enjoy those snacktime breaks in our housework routine. In the back of my mind I still feel jealous of my brothers being always outdoors. But, when we arrive where they are, I am no longer envious when I see how dirty they are! They wipe their hands on their pants and then eat with their unwashed dirty hands! Momma doesn't say one word about that!

After the refreshment break is over, Daddy swallows the last of his coffee and usually says that it is time to "get back to work." But, on this particular day, he adds a second announcement that is quiet different and shocking.

"Family," he began, "we've all been working extra hard this summer. I think we all deserve a vacation! Momma, would you agree with that?"

"Oh, Papa, I do indeed! *Hoch zeit!*" (High time!)

Now, I didn't know what a "vacation" was, so I was ready to listen. So were my three brothers. We all listened intently to the conversation that followed between our parents.

"How does this sound to you, Momma? How about the coast of Texas? We could go to Galveston—or would you rather go to Corpus Christi?"

"Galveston is farther away, Papa. But that beach is my favorite."

"Then it's Galveston! Shall we ask Uncle Ernst and Aunt Sophie to go with us? They would come along, I'm sure."

"Oh, that would be so fun! I'll telephone Aunt Sophie when we get back to the house and ask them?"

"*Ja. Das ist gut.* If they say they want to go, I'll make the arrangements for a place for all of us to stay right on the beach. Yes, sir! It's time for a vacation!"

"*So machen mir das denn. Komm, Puppe! Mach schnell.*"

(That's a good plan. Come, doll. Hurry up.)

Up to this point not one of us kids had said a word. I don't know why my brothers didn't say anything, but as for me, I didn't know what was happening! I've never been anyplace but Fredericksburg and San Antonio and Mason.

I had to run to stay up with Momma. Her steps seemed light and happy and longer somehow.

"Momma, what is a vacation?"

"It means we have lots of work to do to get ready. We'll make lots of cookies, can some meat—like chili, brown beans, make some potato chips—"

Momma stopped so suddenly I bumped into her before I could stop.

"*Puppe?* Why are you looking at me like that?"

"What is a vacation, Momma? And, what is a coast and a beach?"

"Oh, *meine kleine Puppe!*" Momma dropped to her knees right there in the field, grabbed me by both shoulders, and looked very deep into my eyes. "You really don't know! A vacation is getting away for a few days! It's resting from all this work! It's being lazy several days in a row! It's not having to rush around every minute of the day to feed the chickens, or milk the cows—"

"But what happens to all our animals if no one feeds them?"

"Uncle Eddie and Aunt Edna will come—or Opa and Oma will take care of the place while we're gone. Don't worry."

"But Momma, you have tears in your eyes! Why are you crying, Momma?

Momma enfolded me in a huge bear hug. "Oh, *Puppe,* it's going to be such fun to see you and your brothers getting to play like children should for a change. I'm just happy, that's all."

"Now." Momma tweaked my nose. "Do you have any more questions before we get back to work?"

"Just two more, Momma. What is a coast and a beach?"

Momma looked at me again with eyes that registered total surprise and shock. Only a second later she smiled. "You know what? I don't think I'll tell you. I don't want to spoil your first look at the ocean and a beach. Just trust me. You'll love it!"

And with that Momma stood up and gently took my hand, and together we slowly strolled back to the house to continue doing our usual chores. The big difference now was that there was a noticeable lighter step to Momma's walk and she sang church songs with gusto while we worked. I repeated my questions. The only information Momma gave me was one addition for my list of mysterious words. *Ocean* now was added to it. Momma wouldn't even give me a hint. She just smiled and laughed and changed the subject to all we would bake and cook to take with us on our vacation.

Another thing Momma said we needed to do was to make bathing suits for the family. It only added to my confusion and curiosity. What's a bathing suit? Later, I discovered what a bathing suit was and that it was almost like wearing underwear and people were going to see me wear it! Now I was so bewildered I told Momma I could just kick the bucket!

Momma and I cooked brown beans, canned chili, and fried potato chips by the pans full. We packed jars of canned peaches into a box. And then, oh, no, another new word: *Bäcker Brot*. Momma said we would buy *Bäcker Brot* in Galveston for with our meals. Boy! Getting ready for a vacation is exciting stuff!

At last, we are ready. All our cooking and packing of food is finished. The night before we gathered blankets, pillows, sheets, very little personal clothes, shoes, and all the boxes of food Momma and I had fixed. What a mountain! Where would we sit in our Chevrolet?

The night before we were to leave, Uncle Ernst and Aunt Sophie came over in their car. Since they live alone and don't have children living at home anymore, some of our stuff was packed into their car. Very good, I thought, that solves one question for my concerned brain. I also knew for sure now I didn't have to ride with them and be away from my momma when we got to the coast and the ocean and the beach. Oh, and later, my oldest brother went home with them. He would be driving their car for them tomorrow. Things were falling into place.

We left so early the next morning it was still dark outside. Daddy and Momma were excited and kept checking with each other.

"Did you remember to tell Uncle Eddie—"

"*Ja. Ja.*"

"Did you tell them where we would be staying?"

"Yes. Yes."

"Do you have the name of our motel?"

"It's here in my shirt pocket."

"Did you remember to give the extra key to Opa?"

It went on and on until we got to Fredericksburg, then on and on all the way to San Antonio. Once we left San Antonio, both my parents finally seemed to relax. Questions now came from us kids.

"How much farther?"

"When will we see the coast?"

"Can we see it from the car?"

"What color is it?"

Daddy finally promised, "If you would all just go to sleep, time would pass a lot faster."

I closed my eyes and pretended to sleep. Well, maybe I really did sleep—for a while. My eyes snapped open the instant I heard all the shouting and excited cheers, "The ocean! The ocean!" I sat up in an flash and looked out the car window too.

Daddy had stopped on the side of the highway. I saw what they were looking at. It was a long way away. I have never seen anything like that! At first glance it seemed to be kind of a green rolling mass—then blue—then rolling—coming—going away—but not gone! Momma said it was all water! "You are looking at the ocean, children."

I gulped back a lump in my throat. I was not sure I liked this ocean—out there—endless—rolling—never still. I crawled over the seat and into Momma's lap. I wanted to ride up front with her and Daddy. My big brother, Oliver, teased me and called me a baby. He said I was a scardy cat. Warren asked if he too could sit in the front seat. Momma said yes, and now Warren and I were bug-eyed and silent, both sitting there on Momma's lap as Daddy started to drive on.

We drove and drove. It seemed like we'd never get where we'd be on vacation.

Finally, we arrived in the city of Galveston. It was strange because now we couldn't see the ocean anywhere. I asked where had it gone. Was it under us? Were we driving on top of it? Could we fall into it?

I was so nervous I was beginning to feel sick to my stomach. I told Momma and she said I should put my head on her shoulder and close my eyes. Everything was just fine, she said. Just wonderful and fine.

"Pretty soon you are going to be very happy and surprised."

I squeezed my eyes shut really tight and sure enough, it was not long when I felt our car come to a stop. I looked out the window and there it was. The ocean. And, I can't explain why, but now I wasn't afraid anymore and I caught the excitement in everyone else's voices as they rushed around to unpack the cars and carry all our things into a place called a motel.

There were beds inside and a dresser and a bathroom and a table and four chairs. There was a tiny kitchen area with a strange kind of stove. It was certainly not like our wood burning stove at home. Daddy lit a match to "make sure it worked." He held the match to the burner, and a blue flame jumped up when he turned a knob. He turned it off again.

Then Daddy shouted, "Okay, everybody! Into your bathing suits! Let's check out the beach and go jump in the ocean!"

At first I was reluctant to come out where my brothers could see me in my bathing suit. It didn't take long, however, for me to understand that they were not even looking at me—they were laughing and yelling at the top of their voices and jumping up and down and yelling with every rolling wave in the ocean.

Momma held my hand and Warren's too as we walked slowly onto the beautiful sandy beach and eventually into the cold, lapping water. What a sensation! Finally I was able to laugh right along with everyone else. Here I could shout as loud as I wanted. Nobody seemed to care about anything. Momma and Daddy were jumping

Oliver, Warren, Alora, and Aunt Sophie as they discover what an "ocean" is.
— Photo from author's collection

With Warren and Aunt Sophie in the foreground, and Daddy, Otto Jr., and Uncle Ernst in Galveston, Texas. Note Daddy's swim suit.
— From the author's collection

The swim suits worn by bathing beauties. Momma (left) and two of her friends on the Galveston beach in July 1915.

— From the author's collection

around and laughing and hugging each other, and Uncle Ernst and Aunt Sophie were dancing around and around. It was crazy! It was fun! I think I like vacations!

We played on the beach, made sand piles, and gathered a lot of shells.

It was almost dark, and the ocean seemed to calm down and be still. We went back to the motel to shower. That was a first too! Warm water came right out of a faucet up on the wall! It was awesome!

Next, we ate some of the food we'd brought. And I found out what *Bäcker Brot* was. It is bread baked in a bakery, Momma said. It was already sliced! It was so good I ate six slices of it before Momma said I'd had enough!

After dark we sat outside our motel and watched the moon come up. It was the most beautiful sight I have ever seen. It was so enchanting no one said a word for a long time. I saw Momma and Daddy hold hands and smile at each other like they shared a secret.

That night I laid in my bed in the motel, listening to the ocean waves. I felt safe and serene and happy. Being on vacation was a perfect thing to do. Momma and Daddy seemed so happy and carefree. Our farm seemed a long, long way away, and the blue satin headboard never entered my mind.

Chapter Ten

Expectations

Beginning school was a wonderful expectation. Because we go to church every Sunday, I knew all seven kids who will be in my first grade class at our rural school in Doss. I am excited beyond belief.

But one afternoon in late August all my anticipations come crashing to bits. It was a major disaster in my life when we learned I was too young to enter school this year! All the kids in my Sunday school class will be seven years old by September first. My birthday is September twelfth! No state tuition is paid for a child under seven years of age. I missed by twelve days!

I cry and cry and cry! I can't stop. Even the mention of the promised blue satin headboard will not end my tears. It is just outrageous and awful and that is all there is to it! It's unfair! It's wrong. It is the end of the world, and nothing consoles me.

My parents made an appeal to the local school board. After much debate and many visits, they are refereed to the county school board in Fredericksburg. Permission was finally granted for me to enter school, provided my parents pay the tuition for me the first year. I overheard it discussed between Momma and Daddy.

A few days later, Warren and I were outside in the yard playing. I needed a drink of water. Before I could get to the water faucet in the kitchen, I overheard part of their conversation in their bedroom. I don't think they knew I had entered the house.

"Where can we find the money?" Momma said.

"I just don't know. We really can't afford to sell our calves at today's prices." Daddy sounded sad.

"Well, we just can't let this go by without a fight," Momma said and then I heard her say something about needing to get back to her kitchen. I backed out of the kitchen really fast so she wouldn't see me.

I knew I should tell them it was all right if I didn't get to go to school this year. But I couldn't get the words out. I wanted school more than anything I've ever wanted in the whole wide world!

I love Sunday school. I loved church summer school. In June at church school our Lutheran pastor and his wife told us Bible stories and we sang songs in German. There was always laughter there and other kids to play with. Oh, as far as I am concerned, there was no other place like school.

The next day, when I was sitting on the floor in front of Momma in her rocking chair and she was braiding my hair, I really didn't want to bring up the subject again, but I needed to know the truth.

"Momma, what's going to happen. Will I go to school this year?"

"You will go to school! *Puppe?* What makes you think otherwise?"

Momma was done with my hair, and I got up and returned to my knees facing her, my hands clasped in her lap.

"But what if you can't pay the money?"

A shocked look clouded Momma's face. "*Grosse Ohren!* (Big ears!) You've been listening!"

"I couldn't help it, Momma."

"*Ja! Ja!* Well, now you hear this too." Momma scooted to the front of her rocking chair seat. "You will go to school in September, I promise you that. We will find the money."

My tears begin rolling down my cheeks. "Maybe we can finish my satin headboard and you could sell it to help get some of the money."

Momma burst out laughing and hugged me tight, "*Du Dußelkopf!* (You're dizzy in your head). You will go to school and we will not sell your headboard! I give you my word."

Momma stopped laughing and released me from her bear hug. She grabbed me by the shoulders and looked into my eyes just like in the field that day.

"Now, you listen to me very carefully. You are going to school in a few weeks and everything is just fine."

Momma then rocked back in her chair, put her head on the backrest, and looked up to the ceiling. Shaking her head from side to side, she muttered, "*Gott im Himmel! Bitte zeigen Sie mir den Weg!*" (God in heaven. Please show me the way.)

When Momma says and does things like that, I just know things are going to happen. Momma has a certain way of speaking with a determined look in her eyes that just makes you believe that what she says is true! I will, without a doubt, go to school with my friends in September. My Momma said so!

Momma stopped all work on my headboard after that day. All her spare time was now used to make several new dresses for me to wear to school. Some were made out of colorful chicken feed sacks, and one of them was cut out of one of Momma's three Sunday dresses. When I tried to stop her, she said she never liked that style dress anyway.

I love to watch Momma sew. She never uses a store-bought pattern. Together we dream up trimmings for my new dresses that are different and so pretty. Momma also has a button collection, and I am instructed to see how many I can find that are alike. She will use them to decorate.

She also buys me new shoes and socks and store-bought underwear! Momma bought two pencils, a jar of paste, a box of colors, and a red Big Chief writing tablet. Everything except the tablet went into a cigar box. No child on earth could be more thrilled as the beginning of school drew nearer.

Momma spent a lot of money! I don't know where or how the money so suddenly became available. Maybe she sold more cream, or eggs, or chickens. Maybe Daddy sold an extra calf, or sheep, or goats. Maybe he sold an extra load of fire wood. He did that sometimes. I never knew. No mention of money for school was made ever again in my presence or my hearing.

Thus, at almost seven years of age, I am ready to begin school and I am unbelievably happy. A whole new kind of anticipation and a spirit of well-being has entered by life and nothing—absolutely nothing—can dampen my soaring sensibilities.

Chapter Eleven

Gone to Heaven

I began school in Doss in September of 1939. Our rural school is four and a half miles from our home. We live on the furthermost eastern edge of the Doss school district. In good weather Otto, Oliver, and I will walk.

As we begin our walk there are only the three of us. Then, two of my cousins, Erlene and Arthur Lynn, who live on the other side of the main road from our farm, join us. Now we are five. Over a hill the local people call Hahn's Hill, we walk up and then run down. At the foot of the hill lives a family that runs a cotton gin. There are two children there, Lela and Levi. That makes seven. Not quite one-half mile farther are five more children, Marcus, Norma, Viola, Matilda, Robert, and Verdie Mae. A bit farther on are two boys, Lorin and Jack. Almost at school there are three more kids—I don't know them because they're Baptist. Finally, there are eighteen of us! It is all a grand adventure for me. Verdie Mae and I are the only first graders in the group!

In bad weather Otto will drive us to school in our old 1928 blue

Chevrolet. That will be our "school" car, Daddy says. We also have a new green 1939 Chevrolet sedan but, only Daddy drives it!

There are four same-sized rooms in the one-story bungalow school—a very large building. Three are classrooms, and the fourth room has a stage and a piano in it. In my room, called the "little" room, are first, second, third, and fourth graders. In the "middle" room are fifth, sixth, seventh, and eighth graders. In the "big" room are ninth, tenth, and eleventh graders. All twelfth graders are transferred into Fredericksburg High School to graduate.

In each classroom is a huge black round tank-type wood burning furnace with a black stovepipe to take the smoke out through the chimney. On especially cold days we crowd around the furnace to have our lessons.

On two walls are slate blackboards and chalk. All assignments are written on the blackboard for the older kids, and they have to copy them word for word. Then the teacher teaches another class and writes them an assignment on the blackboard. The older kids have to copy the complete question and then write the answers in complete sentences. The "little ones," that's what we are called, are kept busy learning numbers and letters and cutting out things

That wonderful place called school. To learn more about this unique school read A Doss School History in Review 100th Year, Est. 1884. *That book is dedicated to "Miss Edna," the author of the foreword for this book. Miss Edna taught in the Doss schools for twenty-nine years.*

— Photo courtesy *Fredericksburg Standard-Radio Post,* Fredericksburg, Texas drawn on beautiful colored paper called construction paper. Every student in the room stays busy and works at school, just like we are accustomed to working on our farms.

At school there is also music (singing with a piano); art (coloring pictures with our new Crayolas); books (they are not new); a wonderful playground (four swings); and play acting on a stage!

There are girls and boys (not my brothers) who tease me and play with me. There is a serious, stern teacher who is teaching us to count (do numbers) and read and write.

Oh, my, yes! School is pure heaven! A magical, amazing place.

There is a long hall that separates the four rooms—two on one side and two on the other. In that hall, on both walls is a shelf that runs down the full length of the hall, and that's where we must place our lunch, and there are hooks below to hang up our jackets. We must place our lunch and jackets at the same place every day. We carry our lunch to school in honey buckets. Daddy made small holes in the lid with a nail "to give our lunch," he said, "some air."

Momma made us sandwiches with homemade butter, homemade jelly, and homemade bread. Also, every day we have homemade dried sausage which has been stored down in our cool cellar in a huge crock full of lard from last year's butchering. Sometimes we take a tiny jar of our home-canned peaches to eat with the sausage.

Everyone usually has the same lunch, packed the same way—in a honey bucket. But one of my friends, Norma, who walks with us everyday, always has celery sticks! She shares them with me often. I love that celery. She does not like it, she says. I have never eaten celery before. Momma says celery is impossible to raise in our garden and too expensive for us to buy.

When the weather is nice, we all gather under the roof of what is called a tabernacle. It's a large open-air area, covered with a tin roof, and has lots of old benches—I think they came out of the old Lutheran church which is across the street. There's a stage at one end of the tabernacle where a three-act play is presented at school

The students of the "little room" in 1939 at the Doss school. St. Peter's Lutheran Church is in the background. The author is seventh from the left.

— From the author's collection

closing time. It has a roll-up curtain in front of the stage. It is kept rolled up.

After we are through with eating our lunches, we often crawl up on the stage and give pretend plays. Sometimes they are hilarious! Sometimes we form groups and sing songs we've learned at music time. Music time is usually only a few minutes when the entire school gathers together and we sing songs out of a book.

After lunch we go to play games on the large playground area—stuff like Fox Across the River, or we choose up sides for baseball or basketball. Some of the older boys love to play Mumblety-peg with their pocket knives. A few kids play marbles. That sometimes causes squabbles—especially if one boy wins too often and "takes all the marbles"! Mostly, though, we are a friendly mix of young and older students and the environment is most pleasing,

At our school, students are responsible for keeping the classrooms and the school grounds neat and clean. When the weeds get out of control and we've had a shower of rain, the entire student body (sixty kids) pulls weeds during recess. But that isn't work. It's fun with so many kids doing it! The children and our parents take special pride in our school building, our school grounds, and our studies.

On the school grounds we have one tennis court (dirt court); one basketball court (dirt court); one baseball field (makeshift); and there is a teacherage (a small old rock house) where our three teachers live. We play Andy Over There at recess time.

There are no restrooms inside our school building. We have two outhouses instead. One for girls, one for boys. The girls' is a five-holer. One door is private (for the teachers), and the other section has four holes in one long, open section. I hate going in there! It is located at least a hundred yards away from the school building, and that's good because it does not smell too good. At the end of recess

The former Doss school of 1904 became a home provided for teachers in the new Doss school during the author's years here. It is still standing and being used as a lunchroom. It has received a historical marker.

— Photo by Bill Nelson

time we are all herded there by our teacher and told to go. If you did not, well, I soon found out what happens.

One day, soon after I started first grade, I didn't get to go because I'm kind of shy and I didn't push my way in. By the time the bell rang, I had not used the restroom and we had to hurry back to our classrooms or be punished. It was only natural that I needed to go bad during the class session that followed. I held up my hand up as we had been instructed to do if we needed something. The name of my horrid teacher is Miss Olga M. Schmidt.

"Please, Miss Schmidt. I need to be excused."

"You must wait till recess, Alora."

I tried to wait. What will I do? I'm afraid I can't wait!

I held up my hand again. "Please, Miss Schmidt. May I be excused, please."

I was not allowed to leave the classroom! Finally, I couldn't hold it anymore and I peed right there at my desk and soon there was a big puddle under my desk and all around my brand-new shoes.

Of course, I cried!

Oh, the humiliation. And, to make matters even worse, word got around school at recess and I was teased unmercifully. I had to stay in my wet, urine-smelling clothes all day. We also had to walk the four and one-half miles home that afternoon.

As soon as we got home after school, my two brothers thought it very funny and told all of it to Momma. By this time I was so sore and burning between my thighs that I could hardly walk, and I cried as much from hurting as from embarrassment.

I have seen Momma angry before, but never like this! First, she blessed out my brothers good and proper for adding to my misery with their teasing and not calling her on the pastor's telephone. Then Momma, in her gentle way, helped me wash off my legs with warm water and she lightly patted them dry and powered my thighs with baby powder. Next, she called my teacher on our crank-operated telephone. She told her in no uncertain terms, "I am very disturbed and most upset with the way you handled the incident with

Alora today, and, furthermore, from this point on, I am instructing you, Miss Schmidt, to allow Alora to use the restroom whenever she needs it." Momma raged on.

"If Alora ever has another accident and I am not called so that I can get her into clean, dry clothes, you will be looking for another job. Do you understand, Miss Schmidt?"

I am comforted and grateful that my Momma is taking up for me. It took a longer time for me to forgive my brothers and Miss Olga M. Schmidt. But one thing I learned for sure, I will never, never, ever again miss an opportunity to use that outdoor restroom, like it or not, even if I'm late for class! Punishment for being late would be far better than what I endured that awful day and for several days after!

And so we eagerly pursue our education day after day. And then, one day we begin to hear worrisome news from our parents and the older kids. Our German Lutheran pastor has family still living in Germany. I hear only bits and pieces of conversations—just enough to concern me. We are asked in our church to give up coats and blankets and warm clothing to be sent to someplace in Germany to a people called Jews.

My momma owned only two long coats for winter. She gave one of them to the project. Before she did, however, she sewed her name and address inside the pocket lining. She later received a letter written in German from the lady who received her coat. When our Lutheran pastor read the letter to her, Momma cried. I did not understand all the German words, and it was not polite to interrupt, but when my Momma started crying, I left the room before I cried too. I realized it had something to do with war. I planned to keep my ears open for more information.

Later, a project collecting scrap iron was carried out by the students at the school. Two teams were chosen to see which one could bring in the most iron. The scrap iron is weighed as it is brought in and then piled on a large heap on the east side of the schoolhouse. After a few weeks, the metal was hauled away by trucks. It was an exciting contest, and at the same time we felt we had also done

Winning students of the Doss school team in a contest to collect scrap iron to contribute to the efforts of World War II. The large pile demonstrated their deep appreciation for their country and stirred a sincere spirit of patriotism.

— From the author's collection

something personal to help our country. Of course, we didn't really understand. Children seldom do.

We planted two beautiful large pecan trees at school to honor all the young men who were leaving our community to join military service. Mr. Heimann, the principal, told us, "Your grandchildren will play in the shade of these trees someday."

We girls all giggled. The boy's faces turned red.

I like Mr. Heimann. He's our principal. He plays a violin for our assembly sing-along twice a week. I love singing! Music is my special love. Mr. Heiman asked me to sing a solo one morning. I did and everyone applauded. I was so proud! Even mean old Miss Schmidt asked if I would like to sing a solo at our Christmas program. I liked that idea—even if she is mean. Momma says to mind her because she is, after all, my teacher.

So, my world is broadening! There are so many things on my mind these days. I am anxious again for my headboard to be completed. I am sure getting tired of my bed springs being propped up on wooden boxes. I also would like to invite some of my friends from school to spend a night with me. I'll ask Momma on Saturday if we can please finish the headboard.

Chapter Twelve

Saturday Has a Rhythm

But Saturday was not a good day to ask Momma about my headboard. Saturday is a different working day from weekdays. This is the day we must clean house!

Every room has to be done in a particular way. The three bedrooms all need unseen spider webs removed from corners and walls with the broom. Next, the wood floors and living room have to be swept and then oil mopped. We use an oil called O-Cedar. It is red and smells really good—like cedar at Christmas. Momma lets me dust all the furniture and window sills with a rag soaked with O-Cedar. I like that job. Meanwhile Momma begins in the next room.

Cleaning the bathroom is mostly my job because it's so small there's not room for more than one person. I do not like that job. The lavatory, bathtub, and our flush toilet are scrubbed sparkling clean with Dutch Cleanser or, if that is not available, ashes. The floor is scrubbed with a brush, hot water, and home-made soap. Even though it is hard work, I'm grateful we have an indoor bath-

A bathtub from the era of the author's early years. Imagine this—with walls on three sides—and you get the picture of the Hahn family's tiny bathroom.

— Taken at Jingle Beall Farm. Courtesy Susan Rose Durden.
Photo by Bill Nelson

room with a bathtub and flush toilet and, best of all, running water—even if it's cold.

Our bathtub stands up on legs. Momma is not satisfied until even the floor under the tub is scrubbed and clean. That's especially hard, as the tub, standing on four legs, has the bathroom wall on three sides of it and not much clearance of any kind under it. That means I have to lie down flat on the floor to reach into the dark corners under the tub!

Next comes the dining room, kitchen, and back screened porch. Momma and I work side by side now. All the linoleum floors (dining room and kitchen) have to be swept first. Then, all furniture is dusted and rubbed with O-Cedar.

The final cleaning means the linoleum floors are scrubbed with a scrub brush and hot water. Down on her knees, Momma does that. Down on my knees, I wipe up after her with clear, clean water. I have to change water often because Momma says that if I don't, the floors will have streaks on them, and that's not good!

Once the floors are dry, wax is applied and left to dry for fifteen minutes. During that time Momma and I take a breather out on the back steps under the grape arbor. When the floors are dry Momma and I go over the entire floor, again on hands and knees. With soft rags, we buff the linoleum until it is shining and no more streaks can be seen.

When everything is clean, Momma and I put out fresh clean doilies she has crocheted. We fill vases with fresh flowers from our yard. I'm proud of our clean house, as is Momma. It smells special and fresh.

On Saturday afternoon, whether we are expecting visitors after church on Sunday or not, a cake has to be baked. Momma and I spend our resting time, after the house is cleaned, looking for a recipe we want to use. This is always fun. Most of the time she lets me pick. Today I selected a three-layer coconut cake. Coconut is expensive, but we are going to Grandma Lange's house tomorrow and that makes it okay.

Momma is very particular about the steps to baking a cake.

To begin, it is my job to sift some flour three times before she allows me to carefully measure it out for the cake. Finally, I measure three cups of the sifted flour back into the sifter. Then I add one teaspoon salt and baking powder. Now this flour mixture has to be sifted three more times, Momma says. This is important, Momma says, because cake batter mixed by hand must have good distribution of all ingredients. It is absolutely the most important step if the baking is to be successful.

While I am taking great pains to sift the flour three times and not make a mess in our nice clean kitchen, Momma is starting a fire in the wood burning stove. It takes a while, as the heat inside the oven must be just right. My momma never uses a thermometer. She tests the top of the stove with a drop of water. If it dances just right for her, the oven is ready. It's an educated trick to have enough live coals in the fire box to last the entire baking time. It's a definite and an absolute necessity to carefully add only small cuts of wood dur-

Only on Saturday, when the house was sparkling clean, was the farm woman's beautiful embroidery work displayed.

— Courtesy Edna Crenwelge. Photo by Bill Nelson

ing the actual baking. One must not shake or disturb the oven in any way. Otherwise, the cake layers will fall in the middle, and that is a disaster!

Except to my daddy. He loves it when Momma has a baking failure. He always insists that a failure tastes better than a successful, fluffy cake. Momma playfully scolds him when he says things like that. I enjoy watching Daddy tease Momma. They always end in a laughing hug.

But, back to the cake mixing process. Lard has to be measured out in a cup. The lard is from our own rendering from the pig butchered in the winter. It's important to use good-smelling lard, not rancid. To accomplish this, our lard is kept all year in our cool cellar in a stone crock.

So, it's now my job is to go down into the cellar and bring up just enough lard for the cake and enough to coat the inside of the cake pans. It's hard to measure lard into a cup. One must not leave air spaces in the cup, Momma says, as then it will not be a "full" cup. So you take a spoon and press it down—it oozes up over the edge of the aluminum measuring cup, and yuck, you get it all over your hands and arms and, well, you get the messy picture? I try hard to do this right, as even at my young age I understand that we do not waste. If there is even just a tiny bit left over, it is rubbed on the inside of our cast-iron pots.

At last now we are ready to mix up the batter. First the measured lard is dropped into a large glazed mixing bowl; sugar is measured out of our fifty-pound sack of sugar and added to the lard. And here comes the hardest part of making a cake: mixing those two ingredients.

With a large metal spoon, Momma and I take turns stirring and mixing and mixing and mixing and mixing until Momma is satisfied that it is okay. Then, eggs are added, one at a time, and mixed and mixed and mixed again until Momma says stop. Those eggs, Momma says, must always be broken into a small dish first and then given the sniff test. No smelly eggs ever go into our cake! No. They are saved for breakfast!

Next comes the flour mixture and milk, added alternately, and only in very small quantities at a time. Then, here we go again. Mix it. Mix it more. "Mix it at least a hundred times," Momma says. "Count it out. Sing the numbers if you want." The mixing results in a smooth batter. No lumps allowed! Last step, add Watkin's vanilla. Stir some more.

Momma is very emphatic that only Watkin's vanilla may be used. We have a Watkin's man who comes around to our farm and sells not only Watkin's vanilla but all manner of stuff.

His truck is a funny thing to behold. As is the Watkin's man himself. He is almost as big around as he is tall. His truck rattles and clangs and makes a special kind of sound when he's coming up the lane to our house. Even before you can see him, you can hear him. Momma always says, "*Ach. Der Watkin's Mann kommt.* You kids go out and tell him I'll be right there."

It's a sight to behold. His little black truck has double back doors of a little house he has built right onto the back of the little cab he sits in to drive. The sides of it have WATKIN'S printed on them. When he opens those double doors there are "things" hanging everywhere. There are shoe strings, cow bells, brushes with handles, razor strops, bottles of all sizes and shapes, ointments and oils, cough medicine, and so many things!

Then, he lifts up the sides of the little house and props them up with sticks. He shows Momma all the new spices and salves and ointments and medicines he is carrying. Sometimes he even has candy to sell. Momma will not buy that because she knows that before he leaves he always gives each of us kids a black licorice stick. I hate that stuff.

Still, it's an event when the Watkin's man visits. And there's always a squabble about who gets to open the gate for him when he leaves. Usually it's between Oliver, Warren, and me. We make a line in the ground for a starting place and then whoever gets to the gate first gets the nickel. He always hands that person a nickel for opening the gate!

But back to our cake baking. The cake batter is ready to be poured and divided equally into the three greased and floured pans and put into the oven. Momma hates it when they are not of equal heights. And now, Heaven Help Anyone That Stomps Into Our Kitchen! That person will reap the wrath of Momma and me too. Cake baking time is tiptoe time. Momma and I are good cake bakers, and we have worked hard. We will not have failures!

Today's cake turned out especially nice! Icing is Momma's job later on when the layers are cool. Warren and I manage to hang around when it is time to lick the pan. It will win us the right to wash all the dirty dishes after supper!

But, that's okay. I have learned lots of songs at school and I am teaching them to my little brother. We sing and giggle as we wash dishes. It takes us a long time but we have fun. Our favorite song is one I learned in summer school:

Fuchs, du hast die Gans gestohlen;

Gib sie wieder her.
Sonst wird dich der Jäger holen
Mit dem Schießgewehr.

Fox, you stole my goosey gander;
Give him back to me.
Else I'll call the forest ranger,
Who'll shoot you with glee.

After supper on Saturday, it is bath time for the entire family. Our bath water has to be heated in the kitchen on the wood stove in buckets, carried into the bathroom, and then poured into the bathtub. Warren and I can't carry our own water, but it is a rule in our house that you refill the buckets after you empty them, then put them back on the stove to be heating for the next person. And, don't forget to put more wood on the fire or, number one, the fire will go out and the water won't get hot and the next person will be angry and—well—that has happened a few times and my family is not always sugar and pie when someone does not do what they're supposed to do. Funny, though, Daddy never says a word. Momma makes up for him. And another thing about Saturday-night baths, you better clean up after yourself or there will be another problem!

Then comes another Saturday-night ritual. Momma washes my long hair in warm rainwater, then rinses it in rainwater with a little bit of vinegar added. She says that will make my hair soft. After that I sit on the floor on a pillow and Momma sits in her rocking chair and rolls my wet hair onto rags and ties them somehow. I don't know how it works, but tomorrow I will have long Shirley Temple curls hanging down all around my head. Shirley Temple is a little girl about my age who is a singing movie star in a place called Hollywood. Momma says I look just like her, and every time there's a picture of her in our daily newspaper, Momma shows it to me. It is very uncomfortable to sleep this way, but the results are worth the pain. If I can look like Shirley Temple, maybe someday I can go to

Hollywood and sing there too. Funny how many Shirley Temples there are on Sunday mornings at church and Sunday school.

While Momma works with my hair, I work on memorizing my Bible verses for Sunday school. Our Bible verses are printed on what we call "tickets." They are very colorful and elaborately printed in German onto heavy paper and are about one inch wide and three inches long, depending on the length of the verse. The edges of the tickets are scalloped, and we must treat them nice and easy. We don't get to keep it once we've memorized the verse. Next Sunday it will be passed to another Sunday school student.

It is a matter of pride to see how many verses one can recite in our Sunday school class. We get one gold star by our name for every Bible verse we can recite correctly. It is a very important event when we learn them. Lutheran children and parents take great pride in being able to recite Bible verses. I have lots of stars by my name. Not as many as Marjorie Ann, though. She is my best friend, and we always have a contest to see who can get more stars. She has two more than me.

After everyone has bathed on Saturday night, the entire family sits out on the front porch and we talk, or, if we beg Daddy and he's not too tired, we gather around the piano. Daddy plays and we all sing. Hymns usually. We also know a lot of German fun songs. Daddy plays piano by ear, and he is teaching me how to play the bass chords while he plays the treble melody. Great fun, that.

The final Saturday-night thing is listening to the ten o'clock news from our battery radio. There is so much war talk, and while I don't know what that means for us as a family, I do know Warren and I are frightened just to hear talk about it. I know my oldest brother is. Eighteen-year-olds are being drafted to fight in the war.

Daddy was in World War I in France and remained in Germany even after the war was over with the Army of Occupation, serving as a translator. He is very reluctant to talk about his experiences.

"Did you have to carry a gun, Daddy?" Warren is sitting on his lap and asks his innocent question.

Otto P. Hahn, the author's father, taken in 1918 and World War I.
— From the Bernice (Hahn) Dittmar collection

"*Ja. Ja. Das ist richtig.*" He quietly added, "Every man must serve his country." He says it in such an emphatic, strong way that a silence hangs in the air.

"Did you ever kill someone?" Oliver asked.

"I will tell you this. If a fox gets into the hen house and kills your chickens, you must shoot him. In war, when the people of another country arm themselves with guns and threaten to do what that fox wants to do in the chicken house—well. Only difference in our case—it was Americans. So, like I said. A man has to do what a man has to do if he is a good citizen and your country is threatened. Now I will add this. I don't know, if I ever had to shoot at someone, I'm not sure I could do it. About the time I was sent out in the trenches in France, the war was over. I always remember, every day, to thank God it happened that way."

That's the most and longest time my father ever had the floor to speak. We children were all silent after that, and if we had any thoughts we kept them to ourselves. As for me, I noticed how Momma moved closer to Papa while he was speaking. She took his hand in hers, and that's how they remained the rest of the evening. There was no further discussion on the subject. I feel sure that my brother never doubted what will be his response to the military draft if and when it comes.

So tonight my family goes off to bed in a somber mood. Worried about the future, we go each to our own bed. Tonight our family is still intact. Bernice's husband has joined the Navy now, and they are still living in California. He is an ensign, whatever that means.

Tomorrow is Sunday, and as is our custom, we will go to church, and I know for sure I will pray about the bad things that are happening in the world. Momma sighs and comments that the future is always such an unknown blank page.

"Nevertheless," Papa replied, "We are a strong people full of hope."

I trust my papa knows what he's talking about, and I go to bed and frown because of my missing headboard. I remembered then that I hadn't said anything to Momma today about finishing it. Oh, well, now it will have to wait until Monday, because we never work on Sunday. Sunday is a day for rest and church and singing and visiting. Tomorrow we're going to visit Grandma Lange at Lange's Mill. I'll be proud when she sees the cake Momma and I made today.

Chapter Thirteen

Sunday and He Must Be God's Brother

Sunday has its own special rules: Rise and shine! Hurry and do your chores. Sunday school and our Lutheran church is four and one-half miles away, across the road from our school. Our family is never late! Well—almost.

It is the one day in the week when everybody has to make up their own bed! We all take "hurry-up" turns using the bathroom, brushing our teeth, and the usual. My daddy and older brother shave and use hair oil on Sunday and always smell so good. And look good too! They really dress up—white starched shirt with a tie and a suit, even in summer. My daddy also wears a flat-topped bowler straw hat. He really looks handsome!

Momma has taken the rags out of my curls and I feel special too. I love to look at myself in the mirror. I am happy and smiling with my Shirley Temple curls. I delight in swishing my head back and forth to feel my curls swinging from side to side. My brothers love to pull my curls and make them recoil. We laugh a lot on Sunday morning. It is so wonderful not to be working!

Our entire family is ready now—all dressed up in our very best clothes. Momma usually wears a straight, fitted dark dress and always a hat for church. It usually has a veil and a feather. She is wearing gloves too. I love Momma's hats. I am anxious to grow up so I can wear a hat too.

Just before we are ready to leave for church, Daddy gives each of us kids three nickels. Momma ties my three nickels in a corner of a pretty handkerchief. One nickel is for Sunday school, and two are for the church collection plate.

St. Peter's Lutheran Church is very dear to the hearts of Momma and Daddy, and so it is a special place for us kids as well. The church was organized in 1896. My grandfathers were two of the five men to sign the charter and also helped to build it, stone upon stone.

As we drive to church in our green 1939 Chevy, after about one mile, there's Hahn Hill. When you top it you can see the entire Doss valley and our church steeple almost three miles away.

I stare in wonderment at the hand-hewn stone church. It puzzles me how they did it. How did they build that steeple? And how did the cross get way up there on top of the steeple? I've heard the stories over and over how my grandpa and several of his generation hewed the rocks from my other grandfather's place and then hauled them, rock after rock, by horse-drawn wagon to Doss. I try to picture all that in my mind and I cannot. They must have been a sturdy, strong lot.

Church services are in German. There are rumors that we will have an English service every fifth Sunday soon.

Rev. J. M. Bergner, the pastor, came to our Doss congregation in 1936. He is a short, round, vigorous, and jovial man direct from Germany, and all the people hold him in deepest respect and love. He has such a deep voice! We little kids think he must be related to God himself!

St. Peter's Lutheran Church, Doss, Texas. Dedicated September 13, 1896. To learn more about this great church and how it was built, read Die Heilsgeschichte, *St. Peter Lutheran Church, P.O. Box 22, Doss, Texas 78618.*

— Photo courtesy Edna Crenwelge

The tall white altar in our church has gold painted edges and a tall statue of Jesus standing on it. And when Rev. Bergner stands in the tall white pulpit and preaches, his deep voice echoes in the high tin ceiling of the building. It is awesome and a little fearsome.

Men sit on one side of our church and women on the other. I always sit with Momma; Warren sits with Daddy. My two older brothers get to sit up in the balcony with the teenage boys. They often get into trouble because of pranks they pull up there during church services. Rev. Bergner has two teenage sons. They are the ringleaders in a lot of the capers.

Music in our church is played on a hand-pumped organ. The teenage boys have to take turns pumping the organ. The pump handle sticks out of the side of the organ. It really looks funny to see them pump and pump the handle up and down, up and down. Especially if it is a peppy hymn. That is not too often, as Lutheran hymns are mostly slow. The music is very beautiful, though. Sometimes if the song is long and the pumper gets tired, the music from the organ gets slower and slower.

Momma has a pretty singing voice. I have learned a lot of German hymns by just listening to her. Even though I am just beginning to learn to read in English, I cannot follow these words, as the hymn books are printed in German. Momma points to the words while we are singing. I pretend I can read.

I feel good when I'm in church. All our relatives and friends and cousins are here too. It is a very comfortable, safe, and friendly place for a child.

After church, at noon today, we are expected for dinner and to visit my Grandmother Lange at Lange's Mill. Several of my aunts and uncles will be there too.

This is the place where stands the grist mill that my great-grandfather Frederick William Lange bought for $530 in good United States currency in 1866 after the Civil War. It is said that the original cost of the mill in 1864 was $10,000 in Confederate money!

While driving to Grandma's we prod, "Tell us the Lange's Mill story again, Momma, please."

"*Noch einmal.* (One more time.) *Ja! Ja!*" Momma laughs as she begins the story.

"The Langes Landed at Indianola, Texas, in 1854 following a three-month voyage. They came from Bernstein, Germany. They left their homes because the German government and also the church was taxing everyone. The people were already so poor. Too poor to even buy food for their families."

"So how did they get to Lange's Mill?"

"*Du weißt das doch!*" (You already know that!)

"*Ja,* Momma, I know it—but Warren does not!"

"*Das ist nicht wahr!* I do too know it." Warren laughs. "But, tell it again anyway. Please, Momma."

Momma continues:

"They came from Indianola by wagons pulled by oxen and settled in San Antonio. They bought property in San Antonio known today as San Pedro Springs. They were good farmers, and history tells us they had a huge garden and supplied the Alamo, then called Mission San Antonio de Valero, with fresh vegetables and milk every morning.

"The Langes later sold their property in San Antonio and migrated to Doss. They had a particular love for natural springs. The property they purchased near Doss had a wonderful artesian spring that powered a flour mill." Momma's voice reflects pride.

"When your great-grandfather, William Lange, bought the mill, it was already a flourishing business. With the mill so well known throughout the surrounding country and its products so favorable, the Langes immediately realized more power was necessary to handle the growing business.

"A larger dam was built. But, when the dam was completed, there was too much power, and the shaft of the overshot wheel was broken. A turbine wheel was needed to solve the problem.

"The Lange boys left for San Antonio. After a few days shopping, a wheel was purchased from Beyers Mill and the boys started their long trip back home. Carrying the wheel by horse-drawn wagon, it took them four days to travel the hundred miles."

Momma takes a deep breath. "Is that enough of the story now?"

"No, Momma, finish it!" I say.

Momma continues, "When the wheel was in place and ready for grinding, the Lange boys were as happy as could be. They we happy, yes, but so tired from the journey and the hard work, they went to the swimming hole behind the dam to relax while the neighbors came to deliver stacks of sacks of their grain at the mill, ready to be ground the next morning."

"I know what happened next, Momma," I whispered. "That night, a heavy rainstorm came, and the pressure against the new dam made it give way and break, and all the rocks and sand scattered in the rushing stream. Their new dam was gone!"

"*Ja, ja,*" Momma sighs. "That was a most distressing disaster. Not just to the Langes, but think of all the people who were depending on the mill for their bread flour. Everything was lost!" Momma took another big breath and then continued.

"But, brass determination and iron-clad persistence made the Langes decide to build another dam. They began work in 1872. The new dam was completed in 1875. It took them three years! A stone mason, who lived eight miles north of the mill, helped and gave them advice and did his utmost to prove he was skilled in building a dam. He promised it would never break.

"Well, his promise was true. It's still there today! It has been called one of the most remarkable pieces of craftsmanship in the country, built to serve through centuries.

"Do you children remember the sad part of this story?"

"*Ja,* Momma. Go ahead and finish it," Warren said with a lump in his throat.

"In 1878, at the time when possibly all dreams and ambitions had been realized and crops were harvested, F. W. Lange died. He'd had only three full glorious years after the completion of his dam.

The good news is that he willed the grist mill as a token of his life's work to his son, Julius, my father—your grandfather.

"In 1896 Lange's Mill was also officially made a post office named Lange, Texas. My father was the postmaster for eleven years. I was appointed as his assistant until 1915."

After Momma's story ended, we sat back in the car seat and were quiet for a while, digesting what she'd told us again. No matter how many times we've heard the story, we're always very impressed. [The above story is taken from Doss Centennial book co-authored by the author's mother, Clara E. Hahn (nee Lange).]

Julius Lange, the author's grandfather, around 1913. He owned and operated Lange's Mill at then Lange, Texas, from 1878 until his death in 1927.

— From the author's collection

Immediately, when we get out of the car, Uncle Emil asks me, "Lorhen! (He has his own special name for me) *Wie geht's den in die Schule?*" (How is school going?)

"*Ich bin sehr froh über die Schule.* But I have to speak English now." (I am very happy about school, but I must speak English now.)

"*Ach du lieber! Deutsche Studenten sprechen Deutsch! Nicht wahr?*" (Oh, my goodness! German students should speak German! Yes?)

"*Nein.* We are not allowed to speak German at school!"

"*Das ist ja dummheit! Du mußt deine ehrliche geherbinden Eldern nicht vergessen.*" (This is stupid thinking. You must not forget your forefathers and your inherited culture.)

Grandmother Lange, my mother's mother, who is ninety, and

This photo taken with Grandmother and Grandfather Julius Lange on his seventy-fifth birthday.

— From the Warren Hahn collection

mostly bed ridden, has a different opinion. She advocates learning as much as possible in English. I agree with my grandmother.

Momma unpacks our cake first thing, and all of my aunts compliment Momma. Momma always says proudly, *"Die kleine Puppe hat mich geholfen."* (The little doll helped me.)

I never knew my grandfather Julius Lange. He died before I was born. I've seen lots of pictures of him, though. He had a full beard, and Momma said he loved to sit and comb his beard and tell stories. It always makes me sad to look at his picture. I would have so much liked to hear him tell stories. He has such a kind, gentle face. Momma says he was just that, kind and gentle.

Oh, yes! Going to Lange's Mill is a great adventure. Not only because we heard the thrilling story again, but there are, besides that awesome mill, so many neat things here.

After we arrive and have politely said hello to everyone and especially to Grandma Lange, Warren and I sneak away from the rest and go to take a look at another sight. They have this neat outhouse—yes, an outdoor privy, a two holer.

We have outdoor toilets at our school too, and I don't like them at all. But, there was something different about this one. I think it was the way it was built on a steep slope. It sits there all alone, on a sandy trail that wanders through wild flowers. It seems to be suspended—perched, like it was about to topple over!

Warren and I creep up to it. We cautiously open the door. Inside is an old Sears and Roebuck Catalog—so old the pages have turned soft and pliable. There is a clump of daddy longlegs all crowded together in one corner. Later in the day, when it became necessary to use those facilities, I ask Momma to go with me. I'm afraid something will bite me on my bottom or, even worse, I might fall in when I sit down on the open hole!

Being that my grandmother is bed ridden, I asked Momma how she gets up the hill to use the toilet. Momma explains that Grandmother uses a chamber pot beside her bed! I never noticed a pot beside her bed!

I ran back to visit with Grandmother again. I spied it! It looks like a regular chair with a skirt all around it. But now I knew it wasn't a regular chair! It has a pot hidden underneath! A pretty cushion covers the lid.

I was really impressed! I never asked who had to empty it!

There are other things that are interesting about visiting my grandmother Lange. She lives in the strangest house! It has really low ceilings and there are fireplaces in every room. In one of the rooms the door is a half door. You could open only the top half or, the bottom half, or all the way by opening both halves. There are lots of rooms in this house—almost like a maze. It is the original house built on the place. Momma says the room with the half door is where the post office was.

Right next door to this building is a huge two-story rock house. My uncle Emil Lange and his family live there. It is always exciting when all of us cousins go upstairs to look at pictures they keep in a large basket. We use a viewer that holds the picture upright in a slot. When you look through both lenses it enlarges the photo. We look through it every time we come here, yet it never ceases to be exciting.

A Stereoscope gave a three-dimensional view of pictures.
— Courtesy of Antiques On High, Seventh and High Street, Comfort, Texas. Diane Potter, collector

Lange's Mill was built in 1856. It was recognized in 1936 by the State of Texas with a historical marker in observance of Texas' Centennial. Standing today on private property, visitors are not welcome because of past mischief by uninvited guests. Its remains today are only reminders of its glorious past when it was the center of the community then known as Lange, Texas.

— Permission courtesy of Dennis and Shirley Lange. Photo by Bill Nelson

Another thing at Lange's Mill that surpasses everything else is a swing that hangs from one of their many huge cypress trees. It is the absolute height of excitement to see who can swing the highest! Not one of us has ever fallen out of the swing, thank God! I asked Uncle Emil how they got the ropes around the branch way up there! Uncle Emil always laughs and says he climbed up there! Sometimes he says he shot it up there with a bow and arrow! He always laughs when he tells either version. I think he's fooling me.

The utmost and most unforgettable part of visiting Lange's Mill is the awesome artesian spring that gushes out from under a wall of natural rock just below Grandmother's house. This spring flows down the hill to the mill via a four-foot-wide sluiceway to a large retention pond filled with water lilies. The water in the sluiceway flows over probably thousands of small, colorful natural rocks. There is a wooden foot bridge across all of the mill pond that eventually turns into a path that leads up to their barn on the hillside. We are allowed to play and wade in the sluiceway but are forbidden to go to the deep pond with the water lilies.

Beyond the deep pond is the dam that was built back in 1875. Beyond and below the dam stands the mill. We are forbidden to go down to the old mill without an adult. That's okay. We never come to Grandmother's without a visit to the mill. Momma is always willing to walk us through it. I think she enjoys going through it as much as we do. Even though it is no longer a working mill, the ghosts of the past are still there. I can feel them!

It is very, very dark inside the mill and so noisy. One can look down between the thick wooden boards that are the floor of the mill and see water flowing underneath. If we are very, very good and mind Momma, we are allowed to see the water wheel. The rushing, gushing water is an awesome, powerful sound. I stand still and listen carefully. I record it in my ears so I can hear it every time I think of Lange's Mill. What an impressive place for a little child! It must have been fun for Momma to grow up here.

After our visit with Grandmother Lange and all the visiting

Oma and Opa Fred Hahn, grandparents of the author. Note the fine crocheted lace tablecloth.

— From the author's collection

aunts and uncles and cousins, Daddy says we must stop by his parents for a short visit today too. Oma Hahn, my other grandmother, is in her eighties and a totally different kind of person. She is usually seated in a rocking chair, where she constantly rocks and continually swats at unseen flies. She does not talk clearly. She mutters and mumbles and keeps working her false teeth around in her mouth. She talks to herself in words that cannot be understood.

Momma warns us before we stop at their house that we must be nice to her. I am polite, but she makes me extremely nervous.

My father has said often that it makes him so sad to see his mother in such a state. He says Oma used to play the organ in church; that she sang and had a beautiful voice and was a very happy, outgoing lady in bygone days. He said she was known far and wide for her sense of humor. I can't understand what happened to make her the way she is. It makes me sad to hear Daddy talk about her—almost as if she really wasn't here anymore. When we kids ask what is wrong with her, Momma explained to us that she is considered "childish." Everyone seems to take that for granted and that we must accept it as something we all have to live with. I have tried sometimes to just talk natural to her, but she just stares at me until I can't take it anymore and I leave. It is a sad time for Oma.

Now you take Opa Hahn; he makes up for Oma's incomprehensible behavior. He is a boisterous, fun-loving individual, and visiting with him is a contrasting treat.

Opa is a farmer like Daddy, but he is also a county commissioner and known far and wide as a great blacksmith. He has a large shop *(Die Schmiede)* on his farm. It is fun to watch when he has the forge going and is working on a special project. Like today, even though it is Sunday, he is working on something and he didn't mind showing us, for the umpteenth time, all the different tools and how they work—just so long as we stand back and don't come too near to get hurt.

To see him lift a red-hot piece of iron out of the forge and then begin to whack on it with a metal hammer is a sight to behold! Sparks fly in all directions. The ringing of the hammer pounding and shaping the iron on the anvil makes us hold our hands over our ears. It is an awesome thing for a child to behold. He is my grandpa, my Opa!

Opa has a huge two-story barn too and a lot of livestock pens near the blacksmith shop. It seems to me he has the biggest draft horses I have ever seen, and sure enough, they are in the pens today. Sometimes, when my Daddy and Opa shoe those horses, we are allowed to stand outside the pen and watch. But, we must be quiet as mice. We have strict instructions not to mess around at the barn. There is never a thought of disobeying him. We respect his warning.

Along the side of Opa and Oma's large home is a Delco plant that produces lights for their house! This is so amazing to me! I don't understand how come they have such light and we do not.

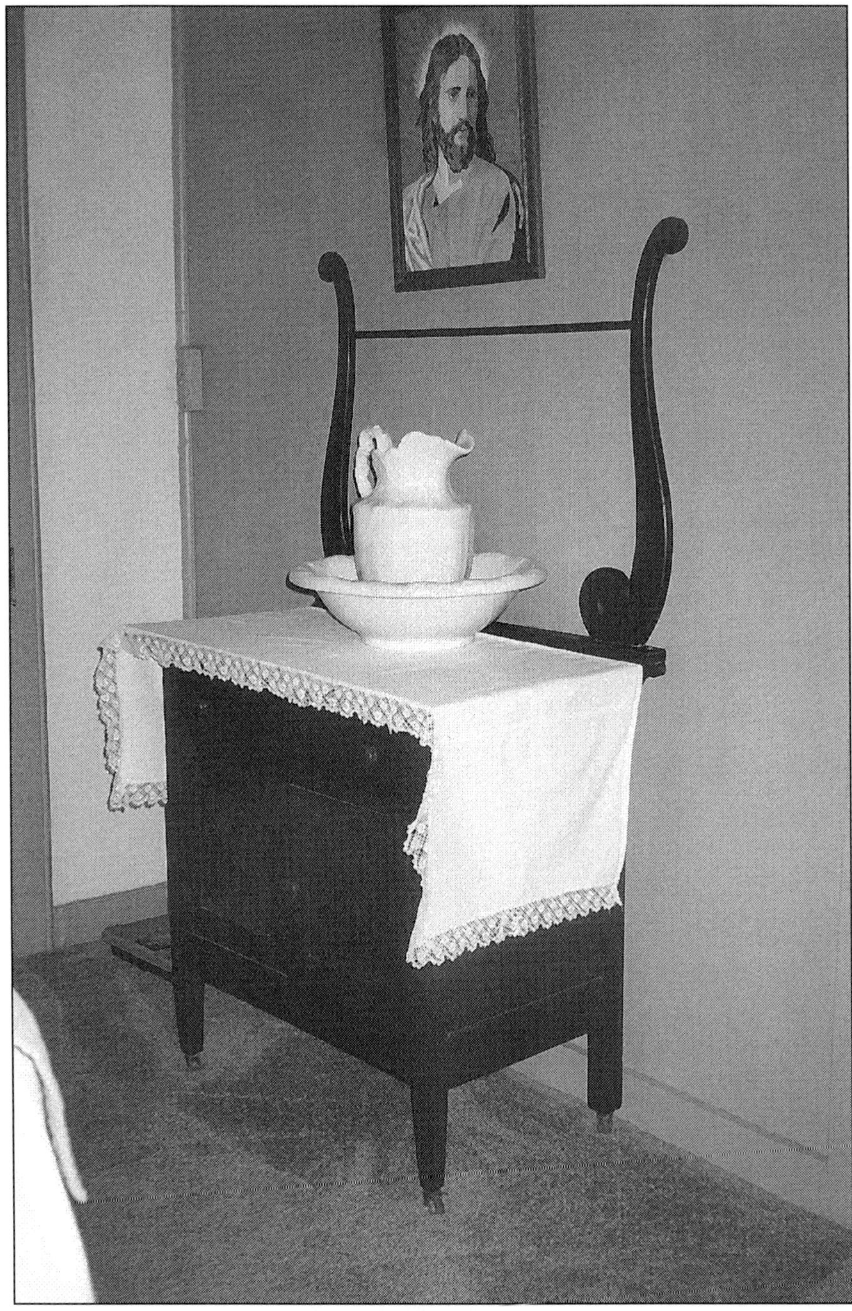

A wash stand like the one in Oma's large bathroom. This one is over 100 years old.
— Courtesy of Edna Crenwelge. Photo by Bill Nelson

A pump organ like the one played by Oma Hahn.
— Courtesy of Edna Crenselge. Photo by Bill Nelson

Momma says it is too expensive for us. We must use coal oil lamps for light.

Opa and Oma have an indoor toilet too, like we do. They also have a bathtub that stands up on legs like ours. But their bathroom is very large! There is also a washstand with a big bowl and a pitcher standing in it. I'm sure glad I don't have to clean this bathroom.

Their house has very large rooms with high ceilings. Oma has her pump organ in the living room, and their furniture is all really nice. I would love to try to play the organ but Momma says I must not touch it. I wonder to myself if maybe, if somebody would play it for Oma … But, when I say something like that to Daddy he just says, "No. I think we just need to leave Oma be."

But now the other thing is, Opa is such a good-natured kind of person who loves to laugh. He walks and sits very stiff and straight. He is a very *stolz* (proud) man, intelligent and respected. Papa says that's his Prussian side coming out.

He has a big bushy mustache too. And oh, how he loves to tease! He has been a county commissioner for many, many years, and he is always involved in local politics. He tells me I should be a lawyer when I grow up! He says I have the "gift." I don't know what that means, but I like it when he says that anyway.

My Opa is so funny. He drives a black 1935 Ford sedan. To back up, he has to press down the clutch pedal with one foot, put the gear shift in reverse, then step on the gas pedal with the other foot and at the same time release the clutch slowly to move the car. Opa never gets it right! When he backs up, he does so with the gas pedal pressed down all the way, the motor races dreadfully, and then the car suddenly shoots backward with a vengeance.

When Opa gets ready to back up, us kids always anticipate the event. We grit our jaws and clench our teeth, knowing what we'll hear. The infamous day when he backed right into one of our fence posts, we all burst out laughing. That was not a good thing for us to do. We were severely reprimanded by Momma later.

Sunday is drawing to an end. We must get home before dark to feed the animals and have a light supper before bed. It has been a wonderful, fun day, and everyone seems rested. Our Sundays are always like that.

Other Sunday afternoons, when we don't go visiting either of our grandparents or have company coming to our house, we usually go for a ride in our new green 1939 Chevrolet. Momma and Daddy enjoy driving us around to different places like Fredericksburg's Enchanted Rock, Balanced Rock, and the granite quarry.

On one of those occasions we found a cut, polished granite rock at the quarry. Since Daddy and Momma were collecting unusual rocks at every opportunity to build a fireplace for our house, we all agreed that that granite rock was perfect for the project. We carried it to our trunk and drove home, at least fifty miles.

After we got home, Daddy said his conscience was bothering him really bad. It could be possible, he said, that particular rock had been cut and polished for a special reason.

"I simply can't have it in our fireplace where I would see it every day for the rest of my life."

We kids tried to convince him that keeping the rock was all right. But, Momma agreed that Daddy was right. So, we all piled back in the car, right then and there, drove the fifty miles, and returned the rock to the exact same place we'd taken it from. When we returned, we all pitched in and had to do our chores by flashlight. But, we were certainly impressed and learned a lesson in honesty.

Chapter Fourteen

Christmas 1939

Monday morning. I am sitting on the floor and Momma is brushing and combing out what is left of my Shirley Temple curls. Although she is being very gentle, it still hurts my head to get all the tangles out. While she is doing this, we talk about Christmas. We will soon be out of school for our holiday vacation, and Momma says as soon as possible we must finish my headboard. Momma has not been able to work on it since I started school.

Momma has been busy making fruit cake and cookies. She makes at least twelve different kinds of cookies. Daddy loves to tease her by stealing a cookie when he passes through the kitchen. They are always at one another verbally, but there is always laughter just beneath the surface.

Momma has been cleaning and cleaning too. It is a must that before Christmas comes all our windows need to be washed and the curtains taken down and washed and starched and ironed. The house must be spotless, because we always have lots of company during the holidays.

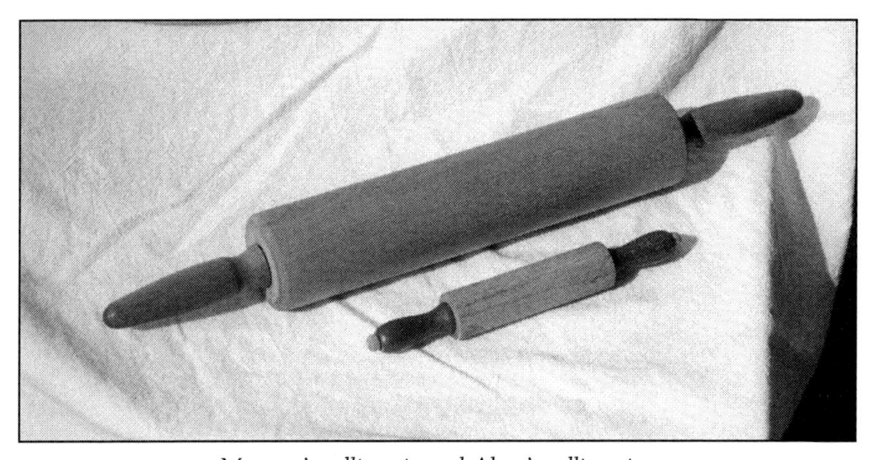

Momma's rolling pin and Alora's rolling pin.
— Courtesy of and photo by Bill Nelson

Momma also says that this coming weekend, on Saturday, Oliver and I must clean the yard to get ready for Santa Claus!

"Momma! I don't mind cleaning the yard—but you said we must also finish my headboard? How can we do both? We have to get it out of the living room so Santa Claus can bring in the Christmas tree."

"*Ja. Ja. Ich wiess das.* We can do both. There is not much left to do except to sew the final seam at the bottom of the satin and add the buttons."

"I'll be so glad when it's back in my room. Momma, I saw Daddy working on our Christmas tree. It is so pretty."

My daddy always finds a cedar tree growing on our farm that will become our *Tannenbaum*. He then makes it flawless by inserting more branches into the trunk. When he deems the tree perfected, he carries it into the living room and then locks all three doors. He says that's the only way Santa Claus will come to leave gifts.

Momma is through plaiting my hair, and finally I am ready for school. Otto is driving us today because we are supposed to be at school early to practice our Christmas program. Miss Schmidt has asked me to sing a special song. She says my voice is pretty. I will try hard to sing loud enough so everybody can hear me.

There are a lot of people that come to our school's Christmas program. They sit on benches in the room with the stage and in the "big kids room." Two side-by-side slate blackboards divide those two rooms and can be raised. That way we almost have an auditorium.

On the floor, in front of the stage, someone has set up a big Christmas tree. The older kids in the big room get to decorate it. We little kids made some of the decorations. We have also drawn names in our room to exchange gifts with one other person. Momma says I must give Miss Olga M. Schmidt a gift too. She has been very nice to me since my accident, and so I guess Momma is right about the present. She really is a good teacher.

At recess time we whisper to our special friends that we are giving each other a present too. Edmund says he's going to give me a bracelet. I told Momma and she said that if he does, I'll have to give it back. Momma says nice little girls don't accept gifts from boys. I'm really sorry about that because I think Edmund is cute.

Miss Schmidt is ready to play the piano for me when we get to school Monday morning. She tells me to stand up on the stage to practice. I am really nervous, but she is playing and I begin singing at the right time.

Up on the housetop reindeer pause.
Out jumps good old Santa Claus.
Down through the chimney with lots of toys.
All for the little ones, Christmas joys . . .

Some of the older school boys come into their room while I'm singing, and since the blackboards are already up to allow the heat from the big wood furnace to warm up the stage room for tonight, the boys hang on the open divider and make faces at me. Miss Schmidt tells them to stop and to go back outside. They don't, mumbling something about "—mean person." She says I should sing it through one more time.

I wish those big boys would leave! This is the first time I've ever sung by myself on a stage. I like to sing, though, so I try to sound really big and loud. I'll show them I'm not scared. I get halfway through the song when the bell rings. Miss Schmidt and I have to quit and go to our room.

We are having assembly this morning after Miss Schmidt calls the roll. We will practice the entire Christmas program from beginning to end. I will have to sing my song again to the whole school! I am really scared and nervous.

The practice was a disgrace. Nobody paid attention and the teachers got really frustrated. Somehow we got through it. Practicing my song went okay, I guess. Edmund smiled at me.

School was fun today. Everybody is excited about our program tonight. I guess Miss Schmidt knows trying to have lessons today is impossible. We clean our classroom instead so it will be nice when we come back after Christmas vacation.

The day passes by quickly, and Miss Schmidt tells us all to politely remind our parents to please be on time for the program tonight.

When we are home after school, everybody rushes around to get our chores done early. We are having our supper early too so we can all get dressed up in our Sunday clothes. Momma says since I'm singing a special song all by myself, I may wear my new Christmas dress if I promise not to get it dirty. It is made of red velvet with a white collar, and it's beautiful! Momma bought the material at Norman Brothers and sewed it for me. I am getting excited!

Momma calls us to come to supper. I take another good long look at myself in the mirror. I think I look pretty nice. I wish Momma'd had time to fix me Shirley Temple curls. "Oh, well," I sigh.

By the time I get to the table, Oliver and Warren are already there. Yuck. I have to sit in the middle. Momma ties a big cloth around my neck so I won't get my dress dirty.

Everybody is talking and laughing and passing the cream cheese and cornbread around the table. I wish I could skip supper, but I know Momma will not allow that. I must be very careful not to soil my dress!

I take just a little bit of food and try to stay as quiet as possible so no one will notice me.

Oliver does anyway and begins to tease me about being scared to sing alone. He's saying stuff to me like, "Your feet are so big!"

Momma makes him hush and tells him to leave me alone. That amuses me.

"See there." I make a face at Oliver. "Now you're in trouble with Momma."

"Oh, yeah?" He says that as he pokes me in the ribs.

"Das ist jetzt genug, Oliver. Ich will daß nicht nochmal sagen!" (That is enough now. I do not wish to repeat myself again.) Oliver knows it's time to stop.

We finally get through supper, and Momma says we will leave the dishes! I can't believe it! That has never ever happened before! She says she'll just put them in the sink and we'll wash them when we get back from the program.

We all pile into our green Chevrolet. I am getting really scared. My stomach is turning flip-flops and the Schmier Kasse is making me burp and my throat is dry and closing up so I can't breathe. I whisper into Momma's ear from the back seat.

"Momma. I don't feel so good."

"*Nein, nein.* You will be fine. Here is a little piece of chewing gum. That will help you. Just don't forget to take it out of your mouth before you start singing."

When we arrive at the school, there are people everywhere! Daddy has a hard time finding a place to park. Finally, we are all piling out of our car and Momma grabs hold of my hand. "Wait, *Puppe.* I will walk to your room with you." All the kids are supposed to gather in the "little kids' room" before the program begins.

When we enter the school building, there are people milling around in the long hallway. It is really noisy with so many kids and parents. A few parents are hanging around inside my classroom too, and Momma gets busy talking to some of her friends. Miss Schmidt sees me chewing gum and sternly reminds me to get rid of it.

I don't know where to put it. I tug on Momma's hand to get her attention, but she is so busy talking and laughing she does not notice me. I also know that when grownups are talking it is not good manners to interrupt. So I wait patiently by her side. My stomach is really getting upset. What if I have to vomit!

Suddenly the bell rings, and that's the signal for all parents to leave and be seated. All the kids are to line up and march into the room with the stage. Momma gives me a final checking over and I whisper to her about my gum.

She says I should spit it into her hand.

"Thank you, Momma."

"Sing pretty, *meine kleine Puppe.* You look very pretty."

"Thank you, Momma. I will sing as loud as I can."

The program begins with the big kids' teacher welcoming everyone and thanking them for coming. There are recitations from some of the big kids and a few group songs and some special piano numbers by a few students who are taking lessons. Finally it is time for my song. Miss Schmidt smiles at me as she goes to the piano. I am making my way up to the stage. My heart is beating so fast I can hear it in the silence of the room.

By the time I get up on the stage, my throat is tight and my hands are sweating. I feel like I'm going to throw up. Miss Schmidt is beginning to play my song!

I look out at all the people's faces. They are all so quiet and just stare at me! I feel like running off the stage. I spot my momma. She is smiling big time!

"All right, Alora. You may sing your song now." Miss Schmidt has stopped playing and she whispers to me to begin. I hear a few snickers in the audience. Miss Schmidt begins to play again, and this time I begin to sing at the right place.

"Up on the house top reindeer pause—" My voice sounds like it belongs to someone else. But, I continue to sing as loud as I can and try to stay with Miss Schmidt on the piano.

I have too much spit in my mouth, but I sing anyway. At the end I sing as loud as possible.

I remembered all the words! When I am through the parents and kids all clap and clap. The big kids' teacher came up on the stage with me. She says I did really well! I am so proud I start to laugh and cry a little at the same time.

"I was scared," I say to her.

"That's okay. You have a very nice voice. I hope you will sing for us again in assembly when we get back to school after Christmas. You may return to your seat now, Alora. "

Everyone claps again as I scamper off the stage.

After the program, Santa Claus came! He handed out all the presents under the tree. Edmond whispers to me that the little red present is from him. I know it's a bracelet because he told me so. I will keep it in my desk so Momma won't make me give it back.

Each child is given a brown paper bag with an apple, an orange, a candy cane, several cookies, and a cupcake.

This night is as good as it can possibly get.

Back home again after the program, Momma said I had sung so pretty that she and Daddy would wash the dishes tonight. I was so proud of myself I just sat down and ate all the stuff in my brown bag.

After the Christmas program, school was out on holiday until after New Year's Day. It was a vacation from school work, but not from work at home. The morning after, Momma said that as soon as we got through with our regular morning chores, she and I would get busy and complete the headboard. *Wow!* I thought. *Did she say complete the headboard? Wow!*

Momma had already satin-covered the eight big coat buttons I'd found in our old button box. We now set to work to sew them onto the headboard. The first step was to measure and mark the places where the buttons were to be attached. Once that was done, it didn't take long for us to sew them in place. Momma worked from one side of the headboard with a huge, long needle with string and pliers, and then I returned the needle back to her.

I was overjoyed as my pretty blue satin headboard developed. But once those buttons were in place, I almost cried, it was that pretty! It looked just like the picture in the Sears and Roebuck catalog!

Momma and I now turned the headboard upside down so we could whip stitch the final seam at the bottom of the satin pillow-case-like cover. It was almost dinnertime, though. Momma asked if I would set the table and get out the food and have everything ready for Daddy and the boys when they came in for dinner. She promised she could have the headboard finished by twelve o'clock and maybe, just maybe, Daddy would reattach the headboard to my bed frame even before dinner!

My heart was singing, and so was I! No little girl could have been prouder or more willing to do whatever was asked of her. I sang

> Jesus loves me, this I know,
> For the Bible tells me so.
> Little ones to him belong.
> They are weak, but He is strong . . ."

Daddy did reattach the headboard before lunch. He was very proud of the work Momma and I had done. All afternoon, I slipped back to my bedroom door as often as I could just to take one more peek at my beautiful bed.

That afternoon, Daddy also moved the undecorated cedar tree into the living room and locked the doors.

Later that afternoon, Oliver and I were assigned the task to begin the cleaning of our yard. It was always fun to work with Oliver because he was such a comical person. Oliver was not exactly fat, but he was a little overweight. He was also sometimes a little bossy, but nothing could dampen my spirits today.

Our yard was mostly sand in the winter months, and we raked leaves and swept the sand with a broom. About to finish our job, Ollie and I decided to play a trick on Warren. We swept the sand in a smooth path from the back to the front porch. Then Ollie put on Daddy's rubber boots and made footprints on the path. We called Warren.

"Look! Boot prints! Santa Claus has been here!" Ollie's voice reflected much excitement.

Our work was not in vain. Warren was undeniably impressed!

Later on that same day, Daddy stopped us from our yard work and told Oliver and me to go find our three butcher hogs and try to put them in the pen. He warned Oliver that he should not hit at the hogs with a stick like he'd been doing lately. He cautioned Oliver that it might make them mad and they would try to bite us.

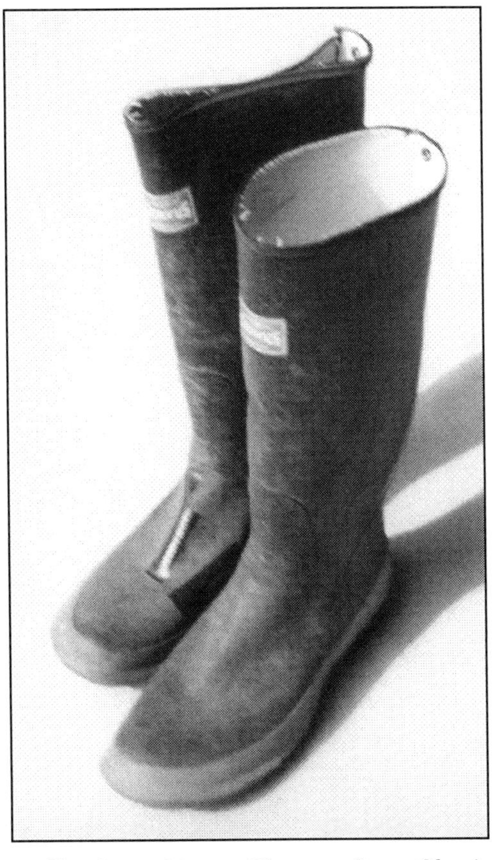

Rubber boots? No, no. These are Santa Claus's rubber boots.

— Photo by Bill Nelson

I was not too sure I wanted any part in this chore, but I figured Oliver was older and he would know what to do. I would just kind of tag along behind.

We found the hogs pretty close to the pen. Oliver was carrying a stick, so I found myself one too.

The hogs were not hard to herd toward the pen. The only problem was there was a water trough between us and the gate to the pen. The pigs decided to stop there and get a drink. Oliver didn't want them to stop. He wanted them to keep going. He took his fairly good-sized stick and hit the lead hog, the biggest one in the bunch, on its back. Immediately, the big hog let out a fierce scream, fell in its tracks, and didn't move a muscle!

Oliver screamed too and cried at the same time. "Daddy! Daddy! Daddy, I killed our hog! I killed our biggest and best hog! I didn't mean to do it, Daddy! I'm sorry! Daddy!"

I don't know where Papa was when Oliver yelled like that but he came running almost immediately.

"Was in die Welt, Junge? Was hast du getan?" Daddy asked. (What in the world? What did you do?)

Oliver showed him how he'd hit the hog on the back, "Like this."

Daddy just started laughing. "Run to the wash house and get a bucket, Oliver. Hurry up."

Well, like I said, Oliver was a little bit fat, and I've never seen him run so fast. He came running back with the bucket.

Daddy dipped some water out of the trough and poured it full force right on the fainted hog. It jumped up—almost in an instant—and ran off rather wobbly, grunting and snorting something fierce. Daddy roared with laugher.

When he was able to speak, Papa explained that a hog has a place like a funny bone on its back and if you hit it just right, well... "Oliver, you must have hit it just right!"

By this time, having heard all the commotion, Momma and Warren and Otto had gathered around us too. Everybody pitched in and helped pen the hogs.

Oliver was on the receiving end (for a change) of lots of jokes out on the porch that night—especially a remark about not knowing he could run so fast!

Out of that event, other stories developed that night. Daddy and Momma have a unique way that sets the scene for storytelling. They never tell us to be quiet. We just know from experience when it is about to happen. Tonight, Daddy began his story.

"Working with animals requires a special knack. Before you can work with them, you not only must let them know you are boss, but there is a trust that develops between a human and an animal.

"Like this afternoon, Oliver. Because of what happened, from now on, every time that hog sees you, he will run from you—for a while. You will have to convince him now that you are not his enemy, but his trusted friend.

"You can get real attached to animals because of that communication between man and beast.

"I will never forget how I felt when some federal agents came onto our farm back in 1929 and shot five of our cows and calves and some of our sheep and goats too."

Momma moved closer to Daddy and took his hand in hers. "It was the one and only time I ever saw you cry, Daddy," she said.

Daddy took a deep breath and shook his head.

"*Ja,* well—I can still see the blood running through the cow pen that day."

"But why, Daddy?" I could hardly speak—my throat constricted with sympathy—not only for my Daddy but for those animals. "Why did they shoot them?" I asked again in a soft voice.

"It's hard to explain. Those were hard times. It was called the Depression—just beginning. Our government thought they were helping us farmers. They shot what they considered surplus animals and then paid us a few dollars for each head they shot. It didn't make any sense then, and it didn't make any sense ever. We were doing all right. We didn't complain. It was those Yankees back east. They didn't have jobs, and they didn't have food or money.

"Some of our cattle from Texas were sent up there so they'd have something to eat. But only a few selected ranchers were given that chance. The rest of us, well, they shot our animals and then paid us a mere pittance for doing it. To make matters even more awful, after they were killed, we had to either burn them or bury them. We could not use any of the meat for food.

"Yes, sir. Our government called it the Agricultural Adjustment Administration. It was set up by the Department of Agriculture.

The whole thing was finally declared unconstitutional by the Supreme Court of the United States in 1936.

"I never did hold with government interfering and telling us farmers how to run our business. We'd do all right if they'd just leave us alone."

Momma and Daddy held hands, as if remembering this demanded that they hold on to each other. We were quiet and thoughtful.

Daddy continued, "That was a terrible time. We were also hit by a drought and windstorms that same year. Nobody had any money. Momma and I had just torn down our old house, and we were in the middle of building a new one when the stock market crashed and the banks closed. We were living in the wash house in the meantime. What little money we had we kept hidden.

"If it hadn't been for Uncle Arnold Lange and other good friends, I don't know what we would have done. Uncle Arnold was a good carpenter, but no one was hiring him or building. He came to help us out in exchange for food and lodging. He had six small children in his family. Yes, sir. Our house is one of the very few built right in the middle of the worst part of the Depression. We thank God for that.

"Yes sir, "Daddy repeated. "I'll never forget it."

Daddy's story was over. He took a deep breath and exhaled. He stood up and flexed his tired back and arms. Then he reached down to help Momma up from the steps of the porch.

"But times are better now. *Nicht wahr,* Momma?" he said.

"And, I also think it's *Bettzeit! Der Weihnactsmann kommt bald. Ja?*" (It's bedtime. Santa Claus is coming soon. Right, Momma?)

"*Ja,* Papa. Morning comes soon enough."

We all did likewise. We all stood up and stretched. Everybody had to walk through my bedroom from the porch because the living room door was locked for Santa Claus. I would spend my first night in my new satin headboard bed!

I asked everyone, gesturing grandly to my bed, "*Ist das nicht schön!*"

"*Das ist sehr schön!*" (That is absolutely beautiful!) Daddy commented.

My three brothers exchanged glances and made funny faces and rolled their eyes at me! I think they might be just a little jealous of my fancy bed! Nevertheless, sleeping in my bed that night was delicious—a quiet satisfaction. Before blowing out the flame of my bedside kerosene lamp, I went to Momma's bed and gave her a big, big hug.

"*Danke shön,* Momma. I will treasure my bed forever and forever."

Chapter Fifteen

Too Young to Understand

And so the 1939 Christmas season came. My sister and her husband came home to visit, and it was wonderful to see her again. They brought presents for all of us, and Bernice could not believe the pretty bed Momma and I had made.

She and Art were to sleep in my bed, and I was proud to let them. But sometime during the day, Otto and Oliver planned a trick on them. They tied a big cow bell under my bed (onto the bed springs) so every time they moved the cowbell would dong! They had dreamed up the prank and wired it so securely that the only way Bernice and Art could stop the clanging was to stuff the bell with Art's socks.

I slept on the cot in the dining room. There was lots of good-hearted laughter and banter all the time they were home for their visit. When the day came for them to return to California, Momma and I cried a lot, but in spite of the heartbreak, we understood that they had to go back to California and back to the Navy, and live their lives.

Christmas toys for little boys.
—From the Don, James, and Roger Durden collection. Photo by Bill Nelson

The perfect Christmas present.
— Courtesy of Edna Crenwelge. Photo by Bill Nelson

And so, the New Year dawned and life for us went on. I moved back into my bedroom, and Otto removed the cow bell, and life settled down to a normal routine.

I was growing from a beginning first grader to a self-assured little girl who was learning everything that was presented to her. Miss Olga M. Schmidt changed too from a "mean old person" to a "very nice lady." She continued to play the piano and encouraged me to sing. She taught me new songs as often as she was able to find the time.

The only dark shadow across it all was the constant adult talk of war. War hung over us like a dreadful omen, an unidentified mysterious something that haunted my mind day and night. War was apparently something dangerous, out there somewhere. It did not have a face. Many nights the blue satin headboard kept me pacified and quiet, but it did not keep me from worrying about what was going to happen to my family if "war was coming" like all the grownups said. Coming where? To our farm? To Texas? I not could not understand or figure out what it all meant.

And then, war did come, suddenly, "without warning" the grownups said, on December 7, 1941. We sat glued to the battery radio. I saw my father and mother exchange glances, reluctant to show their fears. When we expressed concern, they assured us that Pearl Harbor was in Hawaii—a long, long way away from Doss, Texas!

It is an astonishing thing how my World War I parents shielded Warren and me from the agony that they must have felt. Somehow they always put the "best spin" on everything and made sure we were never left without hope of better things to come.

My oldest brother was not accepted for the draft. He had something wrong with his eyes. He was classified 4F (whatever that meant). I felt sorry for him as he watched almost all of his many friends in Doss leave for the military.

My sister remained in California with her husband still in the Navy. He was promoted to ensign, and how handsome he was in the pictures she sent of him in his dress uniform. We received constant

Alora's classmates in February 1939 with Miss Olga M. Schmidt.
— From the author's collection

letters from her, and as far as Warren and I were concerned, everything was still okay in our little world. The war was still out there somewhere, and life went on and appeared quite normal around us. There were no particular surprises as we continued to attend school at Doss and washed and dried our way through lots of dirty dishes, singing our fool heads off, laughing in between until Momma came to see what was so funny. She would just shake her head and went back to her crocheting.

We knew about rationing of sugar, coffee, tires, gasoline, and other things. But we were not worried. We had plenty of food, like always, since we still got most our food off the farm. Everything was normal.

Until, one day, there came a light!

Chapter Sixteen

Light!

If you have never lived with kerosene lamps as the only source of light after dark, you simply cannot grasp the phenomenon of what was called Rural Electrification Administration and the coming of electricity to our Texas Hill Country farms. A miracle was set in motion when that power brought light to the rural farms of America. I am always amused when restaurants use coal oil lamps for romantic atmosphere. Anyone who calls them "the good old country days" wasn't there.

Before we were connected to the source and as the electric line to our house was constructed, Daddy had an outdoor yard light attached to a very high pole set in our yard. Even though the power had not yet been turned on, Daddy flipped the switch to on and left it in that position day and night. He told us the reason he did that was because no matter where he and the boys were—in the pasture or in the field—when they looked up and could see a light burning it meant that electricity had finally been connected to our farm.

They were indeed out in the pasture one day when they saw the light. Daddy and my brothers jumped in the wagon and drove the horses home as fast as possible! What excitement!

Electric service came to our farm in 1942. For the first time, there was light to see by—to read by in comfort and ease. I could now crawl into bed at night and read! At first Momma and Daddy objected. They said I would ruin my eyes! Well, my gosh! That sure didn't make sense. The eye strain happened when we learned to read by coal oil lamps!

Not too many days thereafter, Duecker Electric of Fredericksburg delivered to our house a new Philco electric radio. The shiny wood-cabinet radio stood forty inches tall from the floor and had push buttons for different radio stations. There was one button that said "television."

Warren and I wanted to know what television was. Mr. Duecker said someday in the near future, we'd be able to push that button and we would not only be able to hear a program but we'd be able to see it as well!

"No! You're teasing us! That's not really true. Is it?" Warren and I poked each other and whispered, "He's cuckoo!"

Even the adults guffawed at such a concept. But the idea of television really didn't matter or impress us that much. It was phenomenon enough that now we had an electric radio and could clearly hear all kinds of programs—not just the news! Before, with a battery-operated system, listening to a radio for fun was forbidden.

Momma at once got interested in soap operas like *Ma Perkins* and *Stella Dallas.* At night the entire family gathered around our new radio and laughed as we listened to *The Amos and Andy Show;* George Burns and Gracie Allen; Red Skelton; Jack Benny; Fibber McGee and Molly; Bob Hope Show; Baby Snooks.

We kids listened to *The Lone Ranger; Sky King;* and *Inner Sanctum.* This caused a problem, as those shows came on at a time when we should be doing our chores! Momma fussed and fumed that too much radio would be the "ruination of all young people!"

On Saturdays I listened to the opera and the symphony while I cleaned house. What wonderful music! I enjoyed turning the volume up really loud. Momma and I disagreed about that often.

Daddy could now listen to the fireside talks with the president of the United States. We all did. We gathered around the radio and listened as Franklin Delano Roosevelt said, "I say it ah-gain and ah-gain and ah-gain. We have nothing to feah except feah itself!"

Warren and I would mimic those words the next day. We stood on big oil drums outside in the yard and shouted out those famous words, "I say it ah-gain ... and ah-gain ..." and then we'd explode with laughter.

Yes. Electricity became a force that elevated our lives to a higher level and consequently lifted our spirits.

And then came the most remarkable of all things wonderful: the manufacture and the availability of electric appliances.

We bought a refrigerator! No more block ice? You could freeze ice right there in your own refrigerator? Can you believe it? We even learned how to make ice cream! We drank lots of iced tea and Kool-Aid!

We bought an electric stove with an automatic heat-regulated oven! No more wood needed to be piled behind the stove. With the turn of a dial came heat so hot we had to learn an entire new process of cooking. Baking was a snap for "professional" bakers like Momma and her *Puppe.*

We bought an electric Maytag washing machine with an electric-driven wringer! Monday became a day to enjoy instead of dread.

Who could believe the electric iron! Our clothes were neater, and Momma could not have been more pleased with that. And so quick to heat up—or burn a hole if you kept it in one spot too long. It was an entire new learning process, but I never heard anyone say they wanted to go back to doing it the old-fashioned way.

There was no end to these wonderful inventions. Money was harder to come by than things to buy. Before long, there were Electric Mixer Masters, for instance. Cake baking took on new aspects! And beating egg whites was now so easy to do and took so much less time!

A wall/crank telephone similar to the telephone in this story.

— Courtesy of Susan Rose Durden and Jingle Beall Farm, Comfort, Texas. Photo by Bill Nelson

Eventually came new dial telephones! No more party lines. We used to be on a party line with eight other families. Our identifying ring used to be two long and three short rings. Even though each family had its own identifying ring, that ring rang in all eight homes. If you were a nosy neighbor you could listen in on all your neighbor's conversations. It was a favorite entertainment for lots of people. While you were talking you could hear one receiver after another click in to the conversation. Sure, we did it too. Now, with the new telephone, only your own phone rang, conversation was for your ears only. Some folks thought the new phones had made life rather boring. Others were overjoyed at the thought of private conversations! Especially young people calling or being called concerning a date!

And then there were rumors that something even more revolutionary was coming. Electric Freezers! Be gone, ye old pressure-cooker canner! It was determined to be safe to freeze vegetables and fruits and cook them to eat when you wanted them. Furthermore, they tasted like "fresh from the garden" even in wintertime. Oh! And plastic became the storage for food containers and replaced jars!

Momma, like most farm wives, was skeptical at first. But Home Demonstration Clubs came into being in Doss, with Home Demonstration Agents employed in each county to teach rural homemakers and give them information and confidence. Momma delighted in learning all the new ways.

Farm-to-Market roads were built! No more of the joke that was our "all-weather" roads. The seventeen-mile trip to our nearest city was no longer the undependable, treacherous trek with all manner of dangers around each corner. We had black-topped pavement all the way into Fredericksburg! We drove it often after the highway was built—just for fun!

My entire family went to the Doss school building at night to watch free moving, talking films brought out by Stroeher and Son of Fredericksburg, a dealer who also delivered gas and oil to rural farms. The Stroehers showed us, via film, there was a great big, wide, wonderful world out there. We could now see on moving pictures what we'd only read about in books. The films were in black and white, and sometimes the sound was so loud it almost burst your eardrums. But, hey! Who cared? And no one dreamed or expected that films would soon be seen in color!

Not long after, we heard that a drive-in theater was opening in Fredericksburg. Of course, when that happened, Momma and Daddy piled us kids in the car and we went to check that out!

It truly was an astounding thing! While it was still daylight, we drove into this wide, open-air space, just outside of Fredericksburg on Highway 87. We, along with everyone else, formed a line of cars sometimes a mile long and waited our turn at the outdoor ticket booth. Daddy paid for everyone in the car, then parked at the nearest speaker contraption, which you could hang inside the front door of your car. It played scratchy music before the movie started. Then, when it was dark enough, the sounds and dialogue of the beginning movie replaced the music and you could watch a Western movie on a huge movie screen from right inside your car! Folks in the back seat complained, but this was modern living! Get over it! Mamma insisted we tale turns sitting in the middle, and that settled it.

At refreshment/intermission time we got popcorn and a soda pop!

Life quickly became so much easier and a lot more fun. Living out on the rural farm was no longer the usual long, lonely, grueling daily grind. There was still a lot of work that had to be done, of course. But, now there were tremendous rewards and goals to work toward.

Even Christmases took on a different kind of atmosphere. While the German *Tannenbaum* (Christmas tree) with wax candles was the most exquisite sight imaginable, and the commingled smells of the cedar and wax candles cannot ever be surpassed, electric Christmas lights were so much safer. It was a sacrifice we learned to accept—until one light burned out and the entire tree was swallowed up in darkness!

"Ja, ja," Momma would say. *"Das ist nicht alles Gold was glänzt."* (All that glitters is not gold.)

Momma never bought an electric sewing machine though. She would not part with the treadle machine she'd had since she was sixteen years old. But with better light and more time, it was now possible to sew really elaborate clothes for me, and Momma did so with a passion. She still would not use a "store-bought" pattern, either. She created outfits for me that were the envy of all my girlfriends. And remember the blue satin material and my absolutely exquisite blue satin headboard? One of the first Christmases after we got electricity, Momma made me a pair of matching blue satin pajamas and a robe. The collars and cuffs of the set were quilted. and the buttons were covered with satin too. Along with that gift, Daddy built a new dresser for me out of an apple box and Momma made a skirt to go all around it—yes, also in blue satin. It was material she said she had saved from the headboard project. I had a hard time believing that. I figured she either went back to the store and bought more material or she'd bought more than we needed in the first place. Who knew? All I knew was that life was just pretty darned good and I was a happy young girl!

Chapter Seventeen

The Passing of an Era

And so, with electricity, an era came to an end and a new day dawned. Growing up those early years left deeply entrenched memories of some very difficult times. We often complained, as is typical with most normal youngsters. Sometimes our parents glanced at us with raised eyebrows and puzzled looks. At least in my family, we were gently reminded that we were in actuality very rich and certainly more comfortable because our parents and grandparents worked much harder and had it much worse than we ever dreamed possible.

My parents did not hesitate to teach us about their "olden days" and the history of our grandparents and great-grandparents. I remember we listened with respectful silence and attention—our German culture demanded that. But I also remember that we could not wait to grow up and find better ways to do things—our German culture inspired that too!

So, that's how I grew up, and I am grateful I can write about those early days from personal experience. Those experiences made me cherish the people around me and the events and all those "things" that are "family." Nothing was handed to any Depression families without a price. Sometimes painful sacrifice was required just to survive. It could have made our generation bitter. It didn't in our community. It just made us appreciative.

I don't mind admitting that my attitude today and the many decisions I must make are still influenced by that past. A lot of people I hear and read about scoff at our Depression-influenced generation. I can only wish them well and wonder how they might have done things differently had they walked in our paths.

And today's teens? I admit, I for one, am actually afraid we might come to regret the "without cost to you" free opulence we shower on you in this wonderful new century of technology. Of course, we want you to have a great life. I can only hope that someday you will try to understand us and be interested in our past and hopefully even regard us with a healthy respect.

And I wish I could give one prophecy—that youth will never again suffer through bad times. But my conviction is that somehow we must all come through some "passage" before we can "grow up" to be responsible, caring citizens.

My momma made very few new clothes for herself. I didn't realize how few clothes she had until many years later, when I was a young mother myself and it was time to go through her closet—after she died. Momma had only three of what she called "good dresses"!

Why did she deny herself new clothes? Why did she do so much for me? For my entire family? Why did she make me work so hard? How could we have been "so happy" not having much of anything in the way of "creature comforts"?

Maybe it was ignorance—we didn't know what we were missing. That could be. But even so, I thank my forefathers and parents for my gentle but firm and loving passage. It was some kind of trip! You were brave people to take us with you.

More Collected Family Stories

Vintage 1998

It has become an annual event.

Since 1988, on Labor Day weekend, my siblings celebrate with a reunion. September 1998 we were all in Longview, Texas, with Bernice, the oldest in our family. She is a widow now. Her beloved husband, Art, died of lung cancer following a long and successful career as a physicist working at White Sands Proving Grounds, in New Mexico in the V-2 rocket research program. He was a pioneer in rocketry and at the center of early advancement in our nation's defense program and later in the space program. He always had a pipe in his mouth and probably didn't know that would someday cause his death. Even so, he died in 1992.

At the beginning of the reunion of my siblings, we took note of the missing links. Art was gone, and so was my colorful brother Oliver. His was the first death amoung my siblings. He died of

The Hahn siblings of this story. From left to right, top row, Alora, Oliver, and Warren. Seated are Bernice and Otto Jr. Memories abounded when reunions were in session.
— From the family collection

leukemia in 1990. He too had been in civil service out in New Mexico at WSPG in a missile and rocket motor testing research lab. We think he may have been overexposed to radiation doing that testing. Whatever the reason, we missed him something awful.

We also felt the vacant spot left by my own husband's demise in 1994, another cancer causality. He too was a pioneer in another field: telephone engineering.

In 1997, I retired as an elementary school children's librarian after twenty-seven years in a field that I loved with all my heart. But I had found love again with a close friend of thirty-some years. I married Bill and he swept me off my feet and encouraged me to do something I always wanted to do: write

So, at our reunion, I mentioned that I was working on an autobiographical work on our mother. I said I had some questions on certain elusive details of the past.

Thus began a vigorous, lively several hours of reliving memories. The stories came like the rush of a small Texas dustdevil. It soon became very obvious to me that any history I would try to write about Momma was also about Daddy. They came to us wrapped in one package, and therefore I include those stories here and record them because I must complete the circle. The stories are written as they were told to me, with no regard to sequence or accuracy.

Early Washing Machines

In response to my questions about the power used for the early washing machine, Bernice remembers an unusual contraption. She described a cypress wood tub and a machine that was used for washing clothes before my time. She related that it was a barrel-type tub that had a shaft affixed in the center. The tub was filled with hot water, and then the lid, which had long, ridged metal fingers attached to its underside, was lowered down onto the tub and attached to that center shaft. The shaft, she said, was attached to a lever which, with pure muscle power, was pushed back and forth, and the agitator was set into motion.

According to Bernice, our parents bought a new all-metal Maytag machine in the early thirties, and while it was powered by a gasoline motor, it was much safer. Wash day still remained a physically hard day's labor and very time consuming. It remained so until electricity came.

Time to Slop the Hogs

Bernice remembered that it had been her job to slop hogs when she was very young, that she was required to carry the slop bucket out to the hog pen and pour it into a wooden trough. Slop was a combination of table scraps and water and whey and all manner of foul-smelling leftovers from cooking. She said it always frightened and upset her because the hogs would crowd around her and she'd spill slop all over herself. She said she finally pitched a fit one day and cried about it to Daddy. In a very short time, he devised a fenced-in area for a hog feeding pen. He built a fence over the top end of the trough so she could then feed the pigs and never come in physical contact with the hogs!

A Serious Funny Story

Otto told a story about when he and Daddy and Oliver were through baling hay and were ready to haul those bales into the barn. The two plow horses, Ben and Felix (Felix had only one eye), were hitched to the wagon for the first time. Since they were used to pulling a plow and not used to pulling a wagon, Daddy said they would need to be trained slowly.

Once the horses were hitched up, the wagon was loaded with only four bales. The horses worked well in hauling them to the barn.

On the second trip, a few more bales were added as a load. All went well, and no problem developed in pulling the wagon and delivering the hay.

And so it went—until the last load. The horses decided that the final load was too heavy and would not move. Daddy urged them on with the whip, and every possible enticement was made to make Ben and Felix move. When nothing worked, and it was late in the day, he decided to build a small fire under them.

He lit a small amount of hay under the horses. The horses pulled away, all right, but only far enough to get their bellies away from over the fire. They stopped short again and refused to move. Now the fire was directly under the wooden wagon! Daddy and Otto got plenty busy putting out the fire before it would spread and the wagon and possibly the entire field got burned!

Indian Cure

Otto told a story about when he was a little boy. He became very allergic to something and broke out all over with a horrible itchy rash. After repeated home remedies did not work, Daddy took him to visit a neighbor who was said to be proficient in Indian cures. Mr. Stout, Otto said, dug up a bunch of different roots and cooked them all together, and when the broth cooled off, he bathed him in the solution. He was healed. Otto did not remember what the roots might have been.

Depression Details

Bernice told about how difficult times were when the Depression of 1929 hit. She said the banks closed in 1932—the year our old house was being torn down and a new one was being built and there was a new baby on the way (your author). Suddenly one day, without warning, no one could get their money out of the bank. A lot of people lost a lot of money. Many wealthy people lost all their money. Some jumped out of windows and committed suicide. Our family kept what little cash money they had hidden at home after that.

It was also during this time that everyone had to turn in to the government all the gold anyone owned. Daddy had very few gold pieces, and he decided to save and hide one gold piece for each child. The government called it "going off the gold standard" in the thirties.

It was also during this period that those outdoor toilets at school were built by the WPA (Work Projects Administration) program. That's how those deep trenches were dug underneath the outhouses by this government-sponsored program. These new outhouses were referred to as "pit toilets."

Following Otto and Bernice's stories about the Depression years, I asked how cash income actually was derived on our farm. According to Otto and Bernice, Momma and Daddy sold eggs and cream, wool, mohair, pigs, sheep, goats, and a few head of cattle.

Daddy also had an injury as a result of World War I for which he collected $19 a month veteran's pension. A lot of money in those days. Otto and Bernice discussed the possibility that Daddy could have had his hernia fixed but didn't because he needed the cash more than a fixed hernia!

Daddy also sold and delivered sawed-up wood to the Doss school for their wood burning heaters. He also sold to several elderly customers around Doss. He also did shearing of goats and sheep for hire.

Monthly bills were doctor bills and the few groceries that were

The one-pound butter mold. A valuable farm product taken to market in Fredericksburg during the Depression.

— Courtesy Edna Crenwelge. Photo by Bill Nelson

store-bought. Mostly our family lived off the land. Only staples, such as sugar, flour, cornmeal, salt, oatmeal, and coffee were purchased.

Summertime meat for our table was acquired by the cooperative efforts of a Butcher Club. One day every week one of the neighbors slaughtered a corn-fed calf and each member came to get a certain cut of meat. Each following week a different neighbor slaughtered his calf, and each week a different cut of meat was provided. By the end of the "need" season, each family had received cuts equal to one calf and not one cent had been spent for beef for the table.

During the early fall months we relied on chicken and sheep and goat meat until deer season came around in November and sausage was made. This was also the time when hogs were slaughtered and hams and bacon were sugar cured and smoked. Venison was dried for jerky, a real treat for most everyone. Sausage was dried and packed into lard and stored in our cool cellar.

This was also the time when lard was rendered from the butchered hogs. This was a specialized project that took all day. It was done outdoors in a black cast-iron pot suspended over a roaring fire. Inside the pot went all the ground-up fat trimmed off the pork meat and rinds from the butchered hog. This was carefully brought to a certain temperature and melted. It was then cautiously decanted through a cloth sieve into five-gallon metal cans and allowed to cool. It was then also stored in the cellar.

This process was dangerous, as lard is very combustible and has a way of "spitting" at the person stirring the rendering fat. Momma always wore a long-sleeved shirt when she rendered lard, and we were not allowed nearby except to keep her supplied with wood for the fire.

Lard left over from the previous year was now brought out of the cellar and used to cook homemade soap. This was another all-day process, except it was cooked in the huge copper kettle inside the wash house. The recipe for homemade soap called for several cans of lye. None of us kids were allowed in the wash house until this project was completed because it was considered so dangerous.

This boiling concoction was poured into a soap box that was as

The same authentic-cast iron pot Momma used for rendering lard.
— From the Warren Hahn collection. Photo by Bill Nelson

large in size as a double-bed mattress and at least twelve inches deep. It was made of cypress wood and lined with cast aluminum. Daddy and Uncle Emil Lange built it and shared it between our two families.

When the hot, boiling, thick liquid homemade soap was poured into this box, it had to cool and "set up" for a week or more. Then, Daddy cut it into large pieces with a metal square. Those pieces were then cut in half again and then were stored on an open shelf in the wash house to dry. One batch of this homemade soap was sufficient for our soap needs for an entire year.

Laughter and Love

There were a few humorous tales that were recounted at our family reunion in Longview in 1998. One was the story of about

Art, Bernice's husband, and how he was the butt of a trick one winter at butchering time at the Hahns'. Art was the son of another Doss family of twelve children.

The story goes that Otto and Daddy were very proficient at shooting the hog to be slaughtered. It took a lot of patience and skill to stand with a gun, in the pen with the hog, and wait diligently for the pig to stand perfectly still—so as not to shoot it any other place except right between the eyes. This was to prevent any part of the animal from going to waste.

Now, Art had boasted to Otto and Daddy that he knew all about how to shoot a hog and wanted to be the one to do it this year. He was granted permission.

On the fatal day, Art bragged that he would not miss because, number one, he was a college graduate of Texas University with a degree in physics, and two, how could he possibly miss when he would simply walk up to the hog, hold the gun right to its head, and pull the trigger?

He did so with a slight swagger. He did put the gun to the hog's head; it stood perfectly still and Art pulled the trigger. The hog grunted, obviously in good health and still very much alive. As it ran around in the pen, Art looked at the gun dumbfounded and muttered something like, "What! How can this be?"

When he glanced up, Otto and Daddy were convulsing with laughter. They had loaded the gun with blanks!

It became an oft-repeated story and never failed to evoke convulsive laughter years and years after the incident.

And speaking of laughter, it was also a yearly joke to see who would be pinned with the pig's tail during the days and days of the hard physical labor that was the butchering process. Neighbors helped neighbors. It was always scheduled during the coldest days of December or January, for obvious reasons, and therefore everyone was dressed in layered clothes and heavy coats. It was a constant source of chicanery to see someone walking around unawares with the pig's tail pinned to his backside, bouncing and swinging with every step!

The coffee mill used as a black pepper mill at sausage-making season.
— From the author's collection. Photo by Bill Nelson

Trickery and laughter were always abundant throughout butchering time. As the sausage meat of pork and venison was mixed and ground, it was dumped by large panfulls onto an oilcloth-covered special table and pushed into one large four-inch-thick block of 300 to 400 pounds of twice-ground sausage meat. Then, a special seasoning mixture of salt, pepper, and salt petre was carefully weighed and measured according to the total weight of the meat and sprinkled over the entire block of meat.

The next process was that many hands now worked the meat to make sure that the seasonings were mixed in and evenly distributed throughout.

Oliver and Alora began this chore, working on opposite ends of the large table. Suddenly Oliver exclaimed, "Oh, no! I've lost my class ring somewhere in this meat!"

Alora quickly went to his end of the table and frantically began to go through all the meat that Oliver had already mixed. Oliver let her go through almost all the meat before he casually announced that he had tricked her. His ring had been safely slipped into his own pants pocket!

Warren now chimed in with another "Oliver" story. He and Oliver were topping corn tops, and Oliver bet him he would get to the end of the row first. Warren worked as fast as possible and won. Then Oliver made Warren help him finish his row yet too. Ollie didn't get the best of Warren, however, as when Warren told Momma and Daddy what Oliver had done, Warren got to go visit with Bernice, his married sister now living in New Mexico, an entire week, and Ollie had to stay home and work!

Another part of our remembered childhood was the annual summer vacations taken to the coast, either Galveston or Corpus Christi. We worked all summer long awaiting the time when all the crops were in the barn and all the fruits and vegetables canned and preserved. Once we were finished, Daddy and Momma asked, "Is everybody ready for a vacation?"

Leading up to this time, Momma and I made all kinds of preparations. We canned meat, usually chili and beans. I made potato chips in deep fat on the stove. We baked lots of cookies and cakes. We set aside jars of canned peaches and other fruits. We took all our food.

We also packed all our bedding and pillows. We stayed in cabins right on the beach that had kitchens.

Those vacations were usually taken along with Uncle Ernst and Aunt Sophie (Momma's sister). I remember them as great and wonderful times, and my fondest memory is of my daddy carrying me out into the deep ocean with the waves just tossing us around. I wanted to be afraid, but Daddy assured me he was not going to let me fall.

One morning, our last morning for that vacation, there was no one else on the beach. We kids ran into the water yelling and screaming with delight at having the beach all to ourselves!

It was short-lived! There were jellyfish! Our laughter turned to screams and we learned a painful lesson. If a beach is deserted, there's a reason!

One time when Oliver and I got to spend a few days with Bernice and Art when they were living in Corsicana—where Art worked at the time—we got bored with city life and decided to create an unusual snack. We made ourselves a sandwich with molasses and onions. It wasn't all that bad!

Epilogue

Yes, her name was Clara Emilia (Lange) Hahn. I always called her Momma.

Momma died of pneumonia as a direct result of breast cancer in 1956. She was a pioneer even then as a cancer patient—knowing the risks, she took radiation treatments in El Paso, Texas, where Bernice and Art lived at the time. She wanted so much to live. She would try anything to accomplish that. That was the way she was.

She was horribly burned by the experimental radiation treatments and became violently ill as a result. She returned home to the farm after the treatments but could never recover her strength and was never well again.

Even though I was now married with two small sons and lived in East Texas, I came home to be with Momma and do what I could to help.

On the day when she began to vomit up blood, her body shaking with chills and fever, Daddy and I called an ambulance out of Fredericksburg. We rode with her inside the ambulance to the hospital in Fredericksburg. I saw her turn her head while we slowly drove down the short lane to the main highway. I think she knew she was seeing it for the last time.

Daddy and I and the family sat by her bedside in the hospital day

The special photo of Clara E. Lange, taken at Alamo Studio in San Antonio, Texas, especially for her sweetheart, Otto Hahn, when he was in the army during World War I.

— From the author's collection

Taken in front of Momma's home at Lange's Mill when she was a young lady. Take special note of the visiting young ladies and their hats. Momma is second from the left.
— From the author's collection

and night. She lapsed finally into a coma which lasted almost thirty days. No drugs would stop her illness and fever. Momma died October 8, 1957, with Daddy crying softly and removing his wedding ring.

Warren and Daddy continued to live on the farm after Momma died. But the sparkle was gone from Daddy's face. It was obvious that to him nothing really mattered anymore.

Daddy told Warren and me often that his "heart just broke" when Momma died—it was the first time he couldn't solve her problems or make life easier for her.

Nineteen months later, May 31, 1959, our whole family was gathered at the farm for a reunion. All the siblings were married by now, except Warren, who still lived with Daddy.

We set up our barbeque picnic supper out under the grape arbor in the back yard. There was the usual storytelling and laughter. After supper Daddy went inside the house, we assumed to use the bathroom. When he didn't return, Otto went to see about him. He found Daddy collapsed in his bedroom. Within twenty minutes, he was gone.

If only pictures could talk. Momma and Daddy before their wedding day, after World War I was over.

— From the Warren Hahn collection

Young Clara and Otto going for a walk. Making plans? Looking toward the future? One can only theorize. We do know they loved life and worked extremely hard for the family they would create.

— From the Warren Hahn collection

Daddy died—they said of a heart attack. I believe to this day that he died of heartbreak. He had watched Momma suffer through a radical mastectomy on her left breast. Then, the radiation treatments that had burned her so badly she was in constant pain. His heart was broken over her agony.

Our sadness was overwhelming for many weeks and months. But working through the grief came this realization: Momma and Daddy left us a priceless legacy of love and a special spirit. There was no money to speak of—just a debt-free farm, a place they loved in spite of all the hard work. Through it all they taught us patience, tolerance, the joy of a challenge, problem-solving, and toughness. They solemnly demonstrated respect for our ancestors, the land,

and our fellow men. They stood firm on the values of an honest work ethic and led us conscientiously and happily to toil at a job until it was completed. They taught us pride in accomplishment.

Along with all that, they led us toward a trust and a faith in a loving God and lived it every day for us to see. If they ever doubted the mercy of God, I never heard them verbalize it.

For thirty-seven years they showed us how a marriage ought to be lived. They never spent a night away from each other until Momma was diagnosed with cancer and consequently went to El Paso for treatments. After she returned home, I often saw Daddy sit by her bedside and hold her hand. She was tired. She had fought the good fight. She was, even now, a brave woman.

And so, even in death, Momma demonstrated quiet patience and a love beyond understanding. She never demanded that I live likewise. She never preached at me to believe her way of living was the only way to live. Quite the contrary, she urged me to try new paths, taste new fruits, experience new adventures. She was a great woman and many years ahead of her time. I owe her my life. And still, I just called her Momma.

The young people of the Doss St. Peter's Lutheran Church Choir, 1912, dressed in all their finery, Otto Hahn is located directly behind the fourth lady in the front row. Julius Lange is seen in the background.

— From the author's collection

Write Your Own Story

What is a Golden Wedding Anniversary?

Do you know someone who has celebrated one?

Find their story. Discover that they love to tell all!

Write it! Your teacher may give you extra credit!

Remember to ask their permission!

Give them a copy. They'll love it!

Ask your own Momma/Papa to tell you about how and where they grew up.

Write it down as part of your own story. Be prepared to be surprised!

Talk to your grandparents and ask them to tell you their own special story.

Write the story they tell. You may be shocked to find it interesting!

What is your own special story? Every person as a story to tell.

Good luck and happy writing!

Questions to Explore on the Internet

What is a grist mill, and what products did it produce?

What was the reason for the scrap iron collection drive in World War I ?

Why does a building receive a historical marker, and what is that process?

Are there historical markers in your area?

How did the farm girls in Doss get to Galveston, Texas, in 1913?

What was the steam pressure canner process used on farms in the 1900s, and how does it differ from today's canned goods processing?

What and when was "the Depression era"?

What is the meaning of *budget* and *barter*?

How did the crank telephone work?

How do today's cell phones work?

What is a co-op, and can you find some that exist today?

What was the Rural Electrification Administration Act?

How did the cream/milk separator work? Is that principle still being used today on our nation's farms?

How does electricity make refrigeration?

Why does cream "whip" into butter?

Have fun with your quest for knowledge!

ALORA (MAE) DURDEN-NELSON retired in 1997 after twenty-seven years as the Comfort School District's elementary children's librarian. Her early writing experiences are: stringer, freelance reporter, and Society Editor for the *Kerrville Daily Times;* in the late 1960s she accepted the task to compile and write the history for the Immanual Lutheran church in Comfort, *With Eternal Glory;* while librarian she authored puppet plays twice a year, every year for fifth and sixth grades and produced them for her Elementary Library Children's Theater project. One play, *The Case of the Easter Villains,* was published in *Plays Inc.* magazine in 1976. Other writing credits are: series of newspaper articles for the Comfort PTA and Voter Registration. She presently serves on several boards, as Public Relations writer for the Comfort Public Educational Foundation and the Bill Gorman Memorial Scholarship Group, and was a member of the Comfort Public Library Board (elected president in 1995), resigning upon her retirement in 1997. Her first retirement-stage writing project was published by the YMCA in 1999—the history of the 1,100-acre Robert's Ranch and its use as Boy and Girl Scouts primitive camping sites, and its use field trip locale for historical, archeological, rock-climbing, and birding adventures. She was honored in 1997 with a Community Builder Award by the

Rising Star Masonic Lodge No. 429 of Center Point, Texas. *I Just Called Her Momma* is her first book published under contract.

Bill Nelson, the photographer for this book, is the husband of Mae Durden-Nelson since 1997. He is a retired architect and has designed many homes and businesses, and the Historical Bell Tower on the Comfort Middle School campus. He is a charter member of the Comfort Historical Foundation; served as a board member of Comfort Chamber of Commerce and on the Bishop's Committee of Comfort's St. Boniface Episcopal Church; and is a twenty-seven year veteran on the Board of Directors of the Kendall County Water District #1. He received the Outstanding Citizen Award from the local Chamber of Commerce in 1995.